The Law and Critical Discourse Studies

This book provides a range of highly accessible approaches from Discourse Studies for analyzing legal language in legislation, documents, and proceedings and in news media reporting.

In this insightful volume, scholars from both Law and Linguistics come together to provide a range of approaches from Discourse Studies for analyzing legal language in legislation, documents, and proceedings and in news media reporting. This book begins with tackling exactly why such approaches are hugely helpful and valuable for understanding the nature of legal language and how it is used. The chapters, written in an accessible manner, show how discourse analysis can be used to throw light on the ideas and values which can be buried in legal language. This book provides a valuable resource for researchers wishing to carry out their own research or for use in teaching.

The Law and Critical Discourse Studies will be a key resource for academics, researchers, and advanced students of law, language and linguistics, discourse studies, sociology, and media and cultural studies. This book was originally published as a special issue of the journal *Critical Discourse Studies*.

Le Cheng is Professor in Guanghua Law School at Zhejiang University, Hangzhou, China. He is Executive Vice Dean of the Academy of International Strategy and Law and Vice Chairman of Cybersecurity Strategy and Law Committee of China. He is Editor of *International Journal of Legal Discourse* and Co-editor of *Social Semiotics*. He has published widely in discourse studies and semiotics, in relation to law and cyber governance.

David Machin is Professor at the Institute of Corpus Studies and Applications at Shanghai International University, China. He works in the area of discourse studies and multimodal analysis. His publications include *Doing Visual Analysis* (2018); *Introduction to Multimodal Analysis* (2020); and *How to Do Critical Discourse Analysis* (2023). He is Co-editor of the journal *Social Semiotics*.

The Law and Critical Discourse Studies

Edited by
Le Cheng and David Machin

LONDON AND NEW YORK

First published 2024
by Routledge
4 Park Square, Milton Park, Abingdon, Oxon, OX14 4RN

and by Routledge
605 Third Avenue, New York, NY 10158

Routledge is an imprint of the Taylor & Francis Group, an informa business

Introduction, Chapters 1–2, 4–7© 2024 Taylor & Francis
Chapter 3 © 2022 Jen Neller. Originally published as Open Access.

With the exception of Chapter 3, no part of this book may be reprinted or reproduced or utilised in any form or by any electronic, mechanical, or other means, now known or hereafter invented, including photocopying and recording, or in any information storage or retrieval system, without permission in writing from the publishers. For details on the rights for Chapters 3, please see the chapter's Open Access footnote.

Trademark notice: Product or corporate names may be trademarks or registered trademarks, and are used only for identification and explanation without intent to infringe.

British Library Cataloguing-in-Publication Data
A catalogue record for this book is available from the British Library

ISBN13: 978-1-032-45413-9 (hbk)
ISBN13: 978-1-032-45414-6 (pbk)
ISBN13: 978-1-003-37688-0 (ebk)

DOI: 10.4324/9781003376880

Typeset in Myriad Pro
by codeMantra

Publisher's Note
The publisher accepts responsibility for any inconsistencies that may have arisen during the conversion of this book from journal articles to book chapters, namely the inclusion of journal terminology.

Disclaimer
Every effort has been made to contact copyright holders for their permission to reprint material in this book. The publishers would be grateful to hear from any copyright holder who is not here acknowledged and will undertake to rectify any errors or omissions in future editions of this book.

Contents

Citation Information vii
Notes on Contributors ix

Introduction: The law and critical discourse studies 1
Le Cheng and David Machin

1 Protecting 'Competition, not Competitors': Antitrust discourse and the
 AT&T-Time Warner merger 14
 Pawel Popiel

2 Applying the principles of *Vivir Bien* to a court resolution in Bolivia:
 language, discourse, and land law 27
 María Itatí Dolhare and Sol Rojas-Lizana

3 Race, religion, law: An intertextual micro-genealogy of 'stirring up hatred'
 provisions in England and Wales 40
 Jen Neller

4 The Magna Carta of women as the Philippine translation
 of the CEDAW: A feminist critical discourse analysis 52
 Gay Marie Manalo Francisco

5 The depoliticization of law in the news: BBC reporting on US use of
 extraterritorial or 'long-arm' law against China 64
 Le Cheng, Xiaobin Zhu and David Machin

6 Is this discursive *Yentling*? A critical study of an RCMP officer's interaction
 with a child sexual assault complainant 78
 Christopher A. Smith

7 'If she asked for settlement money, she must not be a real victim': An interdisciplinary analysis of the discourse of victims and perpetrators of sexual violence   91
Huijae Yu

Index   103

Citation Information

The chapters in this book were originally published in the journal *Critical Discourse Studies,* volume 20, issue 3 (2023). When citing this material, please use the original page numbering for each article, as follows:

Introduction
The Law and Critical Discourse Studies
David Machin, Le Cheng
Critical Discourse Studies, volume 20, issue 3 (2023) pp. 243–255

Chapter 1
Protecting "Competition, not Competitors": Antitrust Discourse and the AT&T-Time Warner Merger
Pawel Popiel
Critical Discourse Studies, volume 20, issue 3 (2023) pp. 256–268

Chapter 2
Applying the principles of Vivir Bien *to a court resolution in Bolivia: language, discourse, and land law*
María Itatí Dolhare and Sol Rojas-Lizana
Critical Discourse Studies, volume 20, issue 3 (2023) pp. 269–281

Chapter 3
Race, religion, law: an intertextual micro-genealogy of 'stirring up hatred' provisions in England and Wales
Jen Neller
Critical Discourse Studies, volume 20, issue 3 (2023) pp. 282–293

Chapter 4
The Magna Carta of Women as the Philippine Translation of the CEDAW: A Feminist Critical Discourse Analysis
Gay Marie Manalo Francisco
Critical Discourse Studies, volume 20, issue 3 (2023) pp. 294–305

Chapter 5
The depoliticization of law in the news: BBC reporting on US use of extraterritorial or 'long-arm' law against China
Le Cheng, Xiaobin Zhu and David Machin
Critical Discourse Studies, volume 20, issue 3 (2023) pp. 306–319

Chapter 6
Is this discursive Yentling? *A critical study of an RCMP officer's interaction with a child sexual assault complainant*
Christopher A. Smith
Critical Discourse Studies, volume 20, issue 3 (2023) pp. 320–332

Chapter 7
'If she asked for settlement money, she must not be a real victim': an interdisciplinary analysis of the discourse of victims and perpetrators of sexual violence
Huijae Yu
Critical Discourse Studies, volume 20, issue 3 (2023) pp. 333–344

For any permission-related enquiries please visit:
http://www.tandfonline.com/page/help/permissions

Notes on Contributors

Le Cheng is Professor in Guanghua Law School at Zhejiang University, Hangzhou, China. He is Executive Vice Dean of the Academy of International Strategy and Law and Vice Chairman of Cybersecurity Strategy and Law Committee of China. He is Editor of *International Journal of Legal Discourse* and Co-editor of *Social Semiotics*. He has published widely in discourse studies and semiotics, in relation to law and cyber governance.

María Itatí Dolhare is Lecturer at the TC Beirne Law School at the University of Queensland, Brisbane, Australia. María is a legal practitioner and academic applying an interdisciplinary approach to the research of different areas of land law.

Gay Marie Manalo Francisco is University of Auckland Doctoral Scholar. Her current research interests include women's representation, informal institutions, and transnational relations.

David Machin is Professor at the Institute of Corpus Studies and Applications at Shanghai International University, China. He works in the area of discourse studies and multimodal analysis. His publications include *Doing Visual Analysis* (2018); *Introduction to Multimodal Analysis* (2020); and *How to Do Critical Discourse Analysis* (2023). He is Co-editor of the journal *Social Semiotics*.

Jen Neller is Lecturer in Law at Manchester Law School at Manchester Metropolitan University, UK. She is interested in broad themes of power, equality, and change.

Pawel Popiel is George Gerbner Postdoctoral Fellow at the Annenberg School for Communication at the University of Pennsylvania, Philadelphia, USA. His research focuses on technology policy, particularly how politics shapes the regulation of digital media and emergent technologies.

Sol Rojas-Lizana is Senior Lecturer at the School of Languages and Cultures at the University of Queensland, Brisbane, Australia. Sol is a discourse analyst researching discrimination, memory, and trauma through a constructionist and decolonial lens.

Christopher A. Smith is Adjunct Research Professor at Carleton University, Ottawa, Canada. His research interests include multimodal critical discourse studies, critical pedagogy in language learning, and English language teaching textbook analysis.

Huijae Yu is PhD Candidate and Lecturer in the Department of Korean Language and Literature at Yonsei University, Seoul, South Korea. Her main research interests are language and the law, language and gender, and queer linguistics in South Korean context. She is also working as a lexicographer at the Yonsei Institute of Language and Information Studies.

Xiaobin Zhu is Doctoral Student with an interest in media representations of international law. Zhu is interested in questions of comparative law and media engagement for power and justice.

INTRODUCTION

The law and critical discourse studies

Le Cheng ⓘ and David Machin

> **ABSTRACT**
> The law, in its majestic equality, forbids the rich as well as the poor to sleep under bridges, to beg in the streets, and to steal bread. (Jacques Anatole François Thibault)

Introduction

The liberal view of the law and legal processes is that they are part of maintaining civil society (Cotterrell, 1984). The law comprises a rational set of rules and procedure that seek to treat all individuals in the same way (Allan, 2001). Here, the law strives to deal with facts, is objective and fair and, in a sense, is above or outside of, or disembodied from, society (Slaughter, 2000). In other words, it should not reflect the interests, motivations, ideas and values of specific parties in that society. It is thought to be a fundamental component in protecting both the individual and civil society. The law, here, involves a claim to provide a system of compromises, on the one hand giving people rights and power to carry on with their lives, but on the other to regulate them from preventing others to do the same (Hayek, 2012).

There are also critical views of the law. For example, a crude Marxist stance is that the law simply protects the powerful and their interests and the capitalist system of exploitation (Holdren & Tucker, 2020). And much good evidence can be presented to make such a case. Global corporations are able to produce systematic misery around the world, seemingly supported by international law (Cotal San Martin & Machin, 2020; Mayr & Machin, 2012). Prison inmates around the world are from poorer sections of society or from marginalized ethnic groups, all trapped in cycles of poverty (Hinton, 2016; Rabuy & Kopf, 2016; Western & Muller, 2013). Sentencing patterns and other processes that comprise the criminal justice system in these societies are highly discriminatory against individuals of lower social economic status (Van Eijk, 2017), whose lives might best be described as difficult and brutish, with highly limited access to education, the employment market, good social infrastructure and other resources as well as to knowledge about the law (Mayr & Machin, 2012). Many studies, particularly in the field of the

Sociology of Law, explore other forms of specific inequalities built into the law, legal processes and decision making (Sandefur, 2008; Seron & Munger, 1996).

Another perspective suggests something slightly subtler. The law, by also offering what in some cases is indeed a set of compromises (Cheng & Cheng, 2012) that can include things like workers' rights and human rights, is one way that the present system appears as legitimate, fair and equal (MacKinnon, 2010). Laws do change as interest groups lobby to re-frame issues, as in cases of civil rights (Martin, 1998) and sexual harassment (Marshall, 2005). In this view, the law and the concessions that it gives can be seen as part of how an economic order maintains its sense of consensus and legitimacy, by also providing some elements of broader rights and protection (Hunt, 1993).

This subtler view, influenced greatly by the ideas of Antonio Gramsci and later by Michel Foucault, calls us to reject both the view that laws exist solely as a system of rational rules, external to society, and that it is simply a top-down instrument of the powerful. Rather, the law interrelates with prevailing and dominant ideas and values about what is acceptable, or unacceptable, conduct and behavior in society (Donoghue, 2009). The law is infused into the microprocesses of society, policed and moralized through the professionals of major institutions, in schools, medicine, news media. The Law may appear as simply a formal instrument that serves to enforce wider consensual ideas and values regarding the boundaries of acceptable and desirable conduct, yet it interrelates with all dominant forms of knowledge and how people are positioned and processed in societies (Turkel, 1990). There may be the possibility for change, but only within existing systems of power (Golder & Fitzpatrick, 2013)

Critical discourse studies and the law

Given Critical Discourse Studies' (CDS) interest in the role of language and communication in the functioning of society, in particular as regards to matters of justice and injustice and the exercise of power and control, it is notable that there has been much less attention to the analysis of the language of law. There is an important and rich body of literature on legal processes emerging from the sub-field of Stylistics known as Forensic Linguistics (Coulthard et al., 2010; Solan & Tiersma, 2004), but this is focused more on dynamics of language use as evidence, and in interactions in legal processes, their fairness and appropriate functioning, rather than on understanding law and its use in the context of wider discourses in societies.

There is also a more modest, yet strong, collection of papers with an interest in law, ideology and language, from a literary and cultural studies perspective in the journal *Law Text Culture*. These look at the representation of law, for example, in fiction, theater, strip-cartoons and personal narratives, usually with an Australian perspective and an interest in indigenous law and experiences of Law. Such work, as with wider work on the Sociology of Law and Forensic linguistics, provide important points of reference for studies of the law in CDS.

From the perspective of CDS, the law, like any form of language, carries ideas and values. The language of the law classifies the world and represents identities and human agency. The law shapes, legitimizes and naturalizes social practices. This language formalizes and naturalizes discourses disseminated by other institutions in society, such as government, the media, schools, welfare, immigration agencies, the family (Fairclough, 1989; Flowerdew & Richardson, 2017; Kress, 1985).

In CDS, as with any other instances of communication, we might want to ask what kinds of things are regulated and how, what is represented as desirable or undesirable? What kinds of freedoms are protected and in what contexts? The law may indeed involve a system of compromises, but what are the details of these? Given the nature of language, we certainly would not assume the law to be some kind of rational code somehow existing 'above' or external to the society where it is applied. But nor might we want to take a crude critical view. As Foucault (1980) argued, we may want to avoid making prejudgments about power, but rather aim to carry out careful investigation of individual situations. The papers in this special edition are all concerned with these kinds of questions, in relation to such specific cases.

For a number of reasons, critical researchers may feel overly cautious about engaging with the law. For one thing, the stylistic features of law are off-putting. It is comprised of archaic words and uses of Latin. We find both words with highly flexible meanings and also where there appears to be excessive attention to extremely precise definitions which in itself can become highly obfuscating (Melinkoff, 1963) leading to long, convoluted sentences that seem to repeat themselves (Bhatia, 1993). Such language is explained by some as being necessary for precision and for technical purposes, but to others such language must be viewed more critically as part of a creation of a mystification of law (Cotterrell, 1984), in part legitimizing the power of both the legal profession and the nature of the legal system as a whole (Galanter, 1974).

Another feature of law that can be off-putting for a researcher beginning to work in the area is its self-referential nature. This relates to how each part can reference, and be legitimized by other parts, suggesting a unified, consistent and logical whole (Goodrich, 1990). In each instance, the meaning of a particular law can seem evasive and immediately spread out to the case law that has built up through its use in the courts. For Cotterrell (1984), this sense of a comprehensive system of law, with its dense language, is part of what helps to bring it a sense of being that is natural, rather than value based. It makes it seem inescapable and inevitable. And it lends to the idea that the practice of law is a kind of 'craft', based on a rational system based on accumulated wisdom of the archive of legal judgments (p18). Our aim in this introduction is to consider how a discourse analyst, lacking specific legal training in domains of the law, can nevertheless ask meaningful questions about the law in regard to the discourses it carries. The papers in this special edition then, each in slightly different ways, show how this can be accomplished in specific cases.

The law as language

From the position of CDS, whatever the style of legal language, it can be seen like any other language. CDS is interested in the functioning of any instance of language in politics and in society as a whole. Language is never neutral, even where, as in the law, there may be a striving to give the appearance of being so. And even the criticism of the obscure nature of legal language could be rather a distraction from how it in fact represents persons, events, causalities, priorities, and responsibilities in words and grammar.

To illustrate what we mean, we start with an example using an extract from one of the agreements from the World Trade Organization (WTO), which forms the legal framework governing members' conduct. This particular agreement is in relation to agriculture and lays out the rules for member nations:

> to provide for substantial progressive reductions in agricultural support and protection sustained over an agreed period of time, resulting in correcting and preventing restrictions and distortions in world agricultural markets

There has been much criticism of the WTO in the context of its policies, designed to liberalize economies, opening them to free-trade. Many see the WTO as simply part of allowing powerful global corporations free reign around the planet, even if national governments see benefits from the influx of foreign capital (Rayner et al., 2008). Setting these aside for a moment, we can look at the language used to represent the requirements of the WTO members in regard to agriculture. The agreement here represents the members as being party to 'correcting' and 'preventing' what are defined as 'distortions' in world agricultural markets.

The use of the word 'correcting' here relates to where members must open themselves to free trade and to global corporations. It is not presented as 'intervening', 'modifying' or 'controlling'. 'Correcting', of course, sounds like a good thing. And in this case, the 'distortion' being corrected, would be situations where national governments seek to protect or subsidize established local systems of production and trade, for example, in the case of small-scale peasant farmers.

In terms of CDS, with its interest in grammar, we can note that 'protection' here is presented as a noun rather than a verb. In CDS it has been shown how using noun forms like this is one way to conceal clear formulations of who is doing what to whom and with what outcomes. The lack of clarity here conceals what exactly is being protected, which in this case would mean free trade and the corporations who benefit from it.

In fact, agriculture has been one the most widely criticized domains of WTO activity (Hartwick & Peet, 2003). Critics have shown how the spread of neoliberal regulation and free trade principles around the planet in regard to agriculture has given unprecedented power to the handful of transnational megacorporations that own and control the global food industry (von Oelreich & Milestad, 2017). This has also led to increasing concentrations of land ownership and given more power to the global supermarkets in regard to pricing and over what is to be produced, where and when (Hamilton, 2018; Holt Giménez & Shattuck, 2011; Lorr, 2020). Agricultural production in Global South countries can be quickly transformed and steered to respond to changing consumer demand in wealthier countries, which may be in part driven by marketing and food trends, such as the rise of demand for soya products and exotic foods. Coming back to the noun 'protection' here, we can perhaps think a little more about what, or who, is being protected. We can better grasp what 'correcting' is taking place, and whose interest this serves?

The language of law exists, of course, not only in such written agreements, obligations and rules, but in the language and documentation that uses them, implements and challenges them, which can go all on to comprise case law. And it also exists in the language about the laws, for example by politicians and in media reports about legal cases. We do not have the space here to look at an extended example of case law for the WTO agreements and its representation in wider texts, but we can look at the language the organization uses itself to present them.

On its own website, the WTO suggests the process brought about by members following these rules:

> leads to a more prosperous, peaceful and accountable economic world' and 'breaks down other barriers between peoples and trading economies.[1]

Such language, as when such agreements are spoken of by politicians or in international trade talks, become part of what laws mean. In this case the WTO agreements are accounted for using the word 'prosperous', which connotes something positive, where things are looking up. But in reality, as critics might argue, such prosperity, or wealth, will increasingly find its ways into the hands of those who have the most power to control the market. And while the WTO chooses the word 'peoples' here, suggesting something positive or 'every-person', this is not quite the case. In practice, it will exclude the small scale rural laborers who have no choice but to adapt to these new global rules and the priorities of the supermarkets serving goods to the tables of the wealthy who live half-way around the world. Yet, such laws, framed by how they are presented within specific discourse, become naturalized and embedded within wider patterns of social, economic and political life.

Other language choices are also important here. That the WTO 'breaks down barriers' between people is presented as a good thing, connoting a kind of unifying of humanity. But in practice, 'barriers' can mean economic protection, stability and self-determination.

What this very brief look at the language used to formulate and present law shows is that choice of words and grammar shape how a thing, process, event, place, etc. are represented. Such choices can foreground and background parts of a process, aspects of a person's identity, or features of a place as we have seen in these examples. This selective use of words in language is a natural part of how we communicate in settings, providing our views on things in the world and as we seek to meet our aims, whether this is buying a loaf of bread or persuading someone to buy a used car from us. In this sense we can ask whether or not legal language uses more or less transparent formulations, what kind of representations of situations in the world, of persons, events and places do we find. Are some elements prioritized or even set aside?

Legal language and discourse

In CDS it is taken that language is used in ways that are largely socially determined (Fairclough, 1989). The concept of 'discourse', which has its origins in the work of Foucault (1978), is one way of grasping the significance of this idea. Discourses are established models of interpretation of things in the world that are linked to different social practices and contexts. Language provides an important route through which these discourses are formulated and shared.

Discourses are socially accepted knowledge about how things work and what things mean. They are rather like stories or explanations that are considered acceptable or even reasonable at a particular point in time in a given society. Discourses are how we organize knowledge and the social practices associated with them. Fairclough (1989) and Van Dijk (1998) explained discourses as kinds of mental models or prototypes that are used as a basis for speaking and writing about the world, and also to use as we interpret what goes on around us. Discourses bring with it the categories of types of social actors and judgments about them, and accepted knowledge about how things are to be done.

In this sense, as Fairclough (1989) argued, whenever we are using language this is done in a way that is socially determined through prevailing discourses. These discourses exist in the minds of people, but are also written into school books, into news reports and into the laws of practice and forms of organization of social institutions, as we saw in the WTO agreements for agriculture. For Foucault (1980), such discourses shape what seems plausible, sensible and important. What lies outside of the logic of such discourses can appear as deviant or irrational, somehow outside of society.

For Kress (1979), our view of the world, the prototypes we carry in our heads, are shaped by the different discourses we encounter as we emerge from children to adults, in the family, in schools, family doctors, entertainment media, etc. This will differ, to some extent, depending on our social and cultural positioning. But it means that the language choices available to us in those settings will be pre-loaded with meanings that reflect the historical priorities and meanings developed for social action in them (Kress, 1979).

In terms of law, we can ask what kinds of terms are presented as given or taken for granted. Of what kinds of prototypes and discourses are these a part? In the context of the WTO agreements above, the language choices must be placed into the wider spread of the ideology of free market neoliberalism around the planet. In the language of the WTO agreements, it is taken for granted that there is need for a correction of former imbalances that are to be corrected by free trade. Free trade is itself presented unproblematically in relation to peace, prosperity and harmony between people. The point here is that language can carry presuppositions, which are based on value judgments that can go unstated.

Such presuppositions run through law and legal processes. When charges are brought against a person, when lawyers carry out legal analysis or a judge assesses a case, this is based on a number of underlying notions relating to things like 'responsibility, obligation, causation and the autonomy of the individual' (Cotterrell, 1984, p. 2). Such assumptions are used as neutral, natural and unquestioned (Cotterrell, 1984; Melinkoff, 1963). Yet, as in the case of the terms found in the WTO agreements above, such notions are by no means natural nor inevitable. They are rooted in a particular discourses and established prototypes. And these may exclude issues and causalities, for example, relating to inequalities in societies that greatly shape how people act, the situations in which they will find themselves. Of course, from the perspective of the legal practitioner, such notions will appear as natural. This is since they are interwoven into the seeming self-sufficiency and comprehensiveness of the law as a system, and through the way that they also appear as common sense as laid out in the prevailing discourses in that society at a particular time.

Scholars looking at environmental law comprise one smaller corner of scholarship where there has been more attention to the law and discourse. These scholars have been interested in how laws shift and are shaped by prevailing discourses about nature and the climate at any time. Here it has been shown how the laws themselves and legal decision-making in regard to protecting the environment are driven, not only by scientific knowledge about natural processes and threats to nature, but by the discourses about these issues held by interested parties at a point in time (Jessup, 2010; Jessup & Rubenstein, 2012), which exist in a struggle for dominance (Bulkeley, 2000).

Jessup and Rubenstein (2012, p. 9) explain these discourses as 'usually condensed into simple, succinct and agreeable storylines', which carry a range of typical turns of phrase, formulations, buzzwords and clichés. Such environmental discourses provide 'rallying points' (ibid) for specific parties. In each case these competing discourses will shape the realm of possibility as what the very nature of environmental issues are, how the problem is defined, and what might be done and by whom (Dryzek, 2007). For example, as discourses have changed in relation to things like acid rain Hajer (1993), the ozone layer Litfin (1994), and sustainability (Aston & Aydos, 2019). In these cases, these authors show, the very legal focus and decision-making is shaped by the prevailing discursive frames of different times.

Such discourses, Aston and Aydos (2019) show, will represent things like 'public interest' and formulate relationships between nature and development in the law in different ways. This means that how the environment should be protected varies in form, where this could be through government administration, public participation or through a kind of economic rationalism, where regulation can be accomplished through processes of marketization. Such research provides an excellent indication of the potential for wider studies into the language of the law and legal processes.

Approaching language in the law as an interlocking system of texts

For discourse analysis, the law as a topic for research can appear as challenging, not only because of the opaque language, but precisely because of its self-sufficient and self-referential nature. While news texts or political speeches, or even social media feeds, appear as more simple cases for analysis of language use, laws seem to always form part of a rational interlocking system. Many of us may assume that interpretation here requires the craft of the lawyer.

What we want to show in this special edition is that, as with doing any form of research found under the broader CDS tradition, legal language quickly appears less daunting where we have a clear research question and when we spend time to familiarize ourselves with the relevant laws. As with the case of environmental law, laws are a fundamental part of the core issues with which CDS has traditionally engaged over time, such as gender, race, migration and other forms of social inequalities. Such laws lay out, in each case, what kinds of identities, issues and situations are to be protected from whom and how. As we have seen, such laws are infused by discourses that shape both what can be said about a particular thing and how it can be said. These discourses, as Jessup and Rubenstein (2012) suggest, provide a set of what can be thought of as feasible 'storylines', which are comprised of elements such as kinds of participants, actions, settings, causalities, evaluations, etc. These discourses are infused into the laws but also into other texts in news, political talk, social media networks. The aim, therefore, is to seek out and analyze the language of law and legal processes that are part of the kinds of instances of social inequality and injustice that are of concern to us.

One notable case at the time of writing has been the way that courts were handling what was being called 'hate speech' and 'misinformation'. This provides one useful example of how we can connect issues of injustice commonly covered in CDS to the law, where such laws form interlocking chunks of text.

The issues of hate speech and misinformation had become more salient at the time of writing with the rise of social media, which had given public platforms to a greater range of voices and notably to far-right ideologies. In CDS, there has been an interest in identifying the nature of some of these far-right ideologies through an examination of the discourse carried by their social media (Dobkiewicz, 2017; Ledin & Krzyanowski, 2019).

In Europe, where one of the authors is presently based, the law that deals with these issues involves two articles of European Law in particular. It is of interest to look at the nature of this language and what acts, participants and issues it includes and excludes. What is the discursive script here?

In the first place Article 10 of the European Convention on Human Rights states:

'Everyone has the right to freedom of expression. This right shall include freedom to hold opinions and to receive and impart information and ideas without interference by public authority and regardless of frontiers'.

Such rights relate to democratic principles, but also to things like freedom of religious expression, the rights to assembly and association (included in Article 11).

In cases where such freedom of expression is seen to be threatened, through hate speech or disinformation, Article 17 of the European Convention on Human Rights, which has been called the 'abuse clause' (de Morree, 2017), can be invoked. This states that a person should not:

'engage in any activity or perform any act aimed at the destruction of any of the rights and freedoms of the European Convention on Human Rights'.

In other words, this Article can be invoked where someone seeks to infringe on the rights of others to freely hold and share their own views, for example on the basis of politics or religion or where disinformation threatens rights and freedoms associated with the democratic process.

Here under Article 17 it could be argued that the dissemination of racist literature presents an attack on the freedom of others. Where a court accepted such a view, this would relate to the notion of the 'duties and responsibilities' that come with freedom and expression (Keane, 2007, p. 645). The defense, however, might evoke Article 10 and claim that such literature comprised the views of a legal political party.

Article 17 has been used against claims denying the Holocaust as a historical fact. Yet, as a number of analysts have shown, the application of these Articles can quickly become more complex and much less clear, once there appears to be less consensus about a particular matter (Keane, 2007). This means that its interpretation has been rather uneven and arbitrary (de Morree, 2017). Looking in detail at the uses of Article 17, Cannie and Voorhoof (2011) argue that there is clearly huge discretion involved in what constitutes the nature of democracy and what constitutes a legitimate threat against it. They note strikingly that the first use of Article 17 was the banning of the Communist Party in 1959 in the Federal Republic of Germany, accepted by the Court as a threat to the democratic order. The point here is that while the wording of laws may remain unchanged, the meaning of them, their interpretation and application, will depend on the prevailing discourses of any context and time.

The challenge for CDS here might be, as in the case of environmental law, to investigate how notions such as hate, democracy and misinformation are treated in applications of these laws. It would not be unreasonable to suggest that some of the greatest threats to democratic principles and individual freedoms in our contemporary world come through the actions and systems created by bodies such as the WTO. What is clear is that what is represented as hate speech in both legislation and more broadly in society tends to be shifting, is always ideological, tends to be used strategically, and is often used in ways that are highly decontextualized (Bouvier, 2020; Matamoros-Fernández & Farkas, 2021; Siapera & Viejo-Otero, 2021).

Cannie and Voorhoof (2011) argue that Article 17 tends to operate at a level focused on some former fear of totalitarian regimes, which reflects the prevalent discourses at the time of its creation, and is less in touch with present everyday society. For one thing, it is out of step with technology in the social media environment, notes Banks (2010), where civic space has fragmented into more discrete networks of connectivity (Bouvier, 2020). Here, managing misinformation takes on a whole different order and is of concern for many kinds of public officials. For example, it is known that most people now get their information about illness through social media influencers who have no formal training and tend to provide, at best, content that is inaccurate (Farsi, 2021; Huo & Turner, 2019). As Assimakopoulos et al. (2017) note, the European Union itself is struggling to produce new definitions of hate speech.

From the perspective of CDS, what is of interest here is not so much that these laws protecting freedom and democracy are outmoded in relation to the nature of the current communications landscape. These laws came about as realizations of discourses, of stories about the world, with their associated elements (actors, ideas, values, etc.) that belong to a socio-historic configuration. And, in this discourse, threats to freedom and democracy came in the form of clearly defined forms of political ideologies such as Nazi fascism and Soviet communism. It was not related to fragmentation of civic society, nor by the dangers posed by global corporations.

Certainly, when we look at these laws, their application in case law, and how they are handled in hearings, hate and misinformation are always formulated through very specific discourses, found also across political communication, news and even in academic research itself. Perhaps most interesting is that 'hate' itself becomes a bad thing across these discourses. One might imagine that expressing one's hate of a system of global trade regulation, which clearly removes freedom and brings in forms of oppression and injustice, should be a good thing. Our point here being that what becomes handled as 'hate' and 'misinformation', as with any other notion in language, is never neutral.

Conclusion

The aim of this special edition is, in the first place, to help foster more work that bridges legal research and CDS. We hope to show how CDS provides a useful way to approach law and legal processes in terms of the kinds of power that they carry in individual cases. As Flowerdew and Richardson (2017) put it, CDS is about debunking claims to authority carried by language in texts, through a process of revealing the details buried in language. And this is problem driven, meaning we are asking concrete questions about how a text represents people, process and events in ways that may well be somehow unjust.

Importantly, this special edition seeks to show how we need to examine and explore the law, both in the context of laws and decision-making, as well as in regard to how this relates discursively to how laws are represented in other texts, in political talk, news, popular culture, and public understandings on social media. What discourses run through them? In the sociology of law, it has long been established that laws and legal processes, while presenting themselves as a kind of higher code, cannot be understood outside of their embeddedness in social contexts (Mather, 2013). From the perspective of CDS, this means that we can look at how language lays out particular priorities in legal settings.

The papers in this special edition allow us to start to explore issues laid out in this introduction. Two papers by Jen Neller and Gay Marie Francisco look at the ideologies present in laws themselves. Jen looks at the discourses carried by the UK's 'stirring up hatred' provisions of the Public Order Act of 1986. While this is intended to advance equality, it carries a range of contradictions in relation to the relative immutability of race and religion, which, she shows, carry a risk of serving to essentialize and entrench divisions. Gay analyses the Philippine Republic Act 9710, presented as a local translation of the UN Convention on the Elimination of All Forms of Discrimination against Women. Analysis of documents and proceedings shows how the Act carries discourses of womanhood shaped by a number of Catholic notions of reproductive health.

Three papers reveal ways that the deployment of law can itself be highly discursive, even shifting away from original intentions. Pawel Popiel looks at legal documents from an anti-trust legal lawsuit against Time Warner, calling into question mergers of megacorporations. Here, the courts make their decision favoring the merger, leaning on a discourse where markets require pure free competition, overlooking that markets dominated by large corporations tend towards increasingly lesser competition. Maria Dolhare and Sol Rojas-Lizana look at how laws in Bolivia created to incorporate indigenous notions of territorial rights nevertheless become deployed by judges which carry more Western legal notions of land control.

David Machin, Le Cheng, and Xiaobin Zhu are interested in how laws are used and known, must always be understood within the prevailing discourses of the moment. They look at the US tactically bringing a case against China for breaking their sanctions against Iran, through its reporting by the BBC.

Two papers show how legal process can be seen as competition, not so much about facts, but between discourses that shape how these are to be interpreted. Huijae Yu looks a legal decision-making processes in a case of sexual violence accusations. She considers the typical discursive strategies taken by representatives of victims and accused, which are based on different kinds of 'rights'. Chris Smith considers police interviews with rape victims, showing tensions of how victims can make themselves heard in the context of dominant discourses of legitimate gendered behavior held by the police.

Note

1. https://www.wto.org/english/thewto_e/whatis_e/inbrief_e/inbr_e.htm (accessed on 3 January 2022)

Disclosure statement

No potential conflict of interest was reported by the author(s).

ORCID

Le Cheng ⓘ http://orcid.org/0000-0002-4423-8585

References

Allan, T. R. S. (2001). *Constitutional justice: A liberal theory of the rule of law*. Oxford University Press.
Assimakopoulos, S., Baider, F. H., & Miller, S. (2017). *Online hate speech in the European union: A critical discourse perspective*. Springer.
Aston, S., & Aydos, E. (2019). Environmental discourses and water Law: A case study of the regulation of the Murray-darling basin. *Sequencia*, *83*, 47–86. https://doi.org/10.5007/2177-7055.2019v41n83p47
Banks, J. (2010). Regulating hate speech online, international review of Law. *International Review of Law, Computers & Technology*, *24*(3), 233–239. https://doi.org/10.1080/13600869.2010.522323
Bhatia, V. K. (1993). *Analysing genre: Language Use in professional settings*. Routledge.
Bulkeley, H. (2000). Discourse coalitions and the Australian climate change policy network. *Environment and Planning C:Government and Policy*, *18*, 727.
Bouvier, G. (2020). Racist call-outs and cancel culture on twitter: The limitations of the platform's ability to define issues of social justice. *Discourse, Context & Media*, *38*), https://doi.org/10.1016/j.dcm.2020.100431
Cannie, H., & Voorhoof, D. (2011). The abuse clause and freedom of expression in the European human rights convention: An added value for democracy and human rights protection? *Netherlands Quarterly of Human Rights*, *29*(1), 54–83. https://doi.org/10.1177/016934411102900105
Cheng, L., & Cheng, W. (2012). Legal interpretation: Meaning as social construction. *Semiotica*, *192*, 427–448. https://doi.org/10.1515/sem-2012-0086
Cotal San Martin, V., & Machin, D. (2020). The legitimization of the use of sweat shops by H&M in the Swedish press. *Journal of Language and Politics*, *20*(2), 254–276. https://doi.org/10.1515/sem-2012-0086
Cotterrell, R. (1984). *The sociology of Law*. Butterworths.
Coulthard, M., Grant, T., & Kredens, K. (2010). Forensic linguistics. In B. Johnstone, R. Wodak, & P. Kerswill (Eds.), *The sage handbook of sociolinguistics* (pp. 529–544). Sage.
de Morree, P. (2017). *Rights and wrongs under the ECHR: The prohibition of abuse of rights in article 17 of the European convention on human rights*. Cambridge University Press.

Dobkiewicz, P. (2017). Instagram narratives in Trump's America, Multimodal social media and mitigation of right-wing populism. *Journal of Language and Politics, 18*(6), 826–847. https://doi.org/10.1075/jlp.19039.dob

Donoghue, J. (2009). Reflections on the sociology of law: A rejection of law as 'socially marginal'. *International Journal of Law, Crime and Justice, 37*(1-2), 51–63. https://doi.org/10.1016/j.ijlcj.2009.03.001

Dryzek, J. (2007). Paradigms and discourses. In D. Bodansky, J. Brunée, & E. Hey (Eds.), *The Oxford handbook of international environmental Law* (pp. 1–15). Oxford University Press.

Fairclough, N. (1989). *Language and power*. Longmans.

Farsi, D. (2021). Social media and health care, part I: Literature review of social media Use by health care providers. *Journal of Medical Internet Research, 23*(4), https://doi.org/10.2196/23205

Flowerdew, J., & Richardson, J. (2017). *Introduction, routledge handbook of critical discourse studies*. Routledge.

Foucault, M. (1978). *The history of sexuality Volume 1: An Introduction* (R. Hurley, Trans.). New York: Pantheon Books.

Foucault, M. (1980). *Power/knowledge, selected interviews and other writings, 1972-1977*. Pantheon Books.

Galanter, M. (1974). Why the haves come out ahead: Speculations on the limits of legal change. Law & Society Review, *9*(1), 95–160. https://doi.org/10.2307/3053023

Golder, B., & Fitzpatrick, P. (2013). *Foucault's Law*. Routledge.

Goodrich, P. (1990). *Languages of Law: From logics of memory to nomadic masks*. Cambridge University Press.

Hajer, M. (1993). Discourse coalitions and the institutionalization of practice: The case of acid rain in britain. In F. Fischer, & J. Forester (Eds.), *The argumentative turn in policy analysis and planning* (pp. 43–45). Duke University Press.

Hamilton, S. (2018). *Supermarket USA: Food and power in the cold War farms race*. Yale University Press.

Hartwick, E., & Peet, R. (2003). Neoliberalism and nature: The case of the WTO. *The Annals of the American Academy of Political and Social Science, 590*(1), 188–121. https://www.jstor.org/stable/i370679 https://doi.org/10.1177/0002716203256721

Hayek, F. A. (2012). *Law, legislation and liberty A new statement of the liberal principles of justice and political economy*. Routledge.

Hinton, E. K. (2016). *From the war on poverty to the war on crime: The making of mass incarceration in America*. Harvard University Press.

Holdren, N., & Tucker, E. (2020). Marxist theories of Law past and present: A meditation occasioned by the 25th anniversary of Law, labor, and ideology. *Law & Social Inquiry, 45*(4), 1142–1169. https://doi.org/10.1017/lsi.2020.23

Holt Giménez, E., & Shattuck, A. (2011). Food crises, food regimes and food movements: Rumblings of reform or tides of transformation? *The Journal of Peasant Studies, 38*(1), 109–144. https://doi.org/10.1080/03066150.2010.538578

Hunt, A. (1993). *Explorations in Law and society: Toward a constitutive theory of Law*. Routledge.

Huo, J., & Turner, K. (2019). Social media in health communication. In J. Bian, Y. Guo, Z. He, & X. Hu (Eds.), *Social Web and health research* (pp. 53–82). Springer.

Jessup, B. (2010). Plural and hybrid environmental values: a discourse analysis of the wind energy conflict in Australia and the United Kingdom. *Environmental Politics, 19*(1), 21–44.

Jessup, B., & Rubenstein, K. (2012). *Environmental discourses in public and international Law*. Cambridge University Press.

Keane, D. (2007). Attacking hate speech under article 17 of the European convention on human rights. *Netherlands Quarterly of Human Rights, 25*(4), 641–663. https://doi.org/10.1177/016934410702500404

Kress, G. (1979). *Language as ideology*. London: Routledge.

Kress, G. (1985). *Linguistic Processes in Sociocultural Practice*, Deakin University. School of Education. Open Campus Program.

Ledin, P., & Krzyanowski, M. (2019). Uncivility on the web populism in/and the borderline discourses of exclusion. *Journal of Language and Politics*, *16*(4), 566–581.

Litfin, K. (1994). *Ozone discourses: Science and politics in global environmental cooperation*. Columbia University Press.

Lorr, B. (2020). *The secret life of groceries: The dark miracle of the American supermarket*. Avery.

MacKinnon, C. A. (2010). The liberal state. In M. Krook, & S. Childs (Eds.), *Women, gender, and politics: A reader* (pp. 293–298). Oxford University Press.

Marshall, A.-M. (2005). *Confronting sexual harassment: The Law and politics of everyday life*. Routledge.

Martin, W. E. (1998). *Brown v. Board of education: A brief history with documents*. Bedford/St. Martin's.

Matamoros-Fernández, A., & Farkas, J. (2021). Racism, hate speech, and social media: A systematic review and critique. *Television & New Media*, *22*(2), 205–224. https://doi.org/10.1177/1527476420982230

Mather, L. (2013). Law and society. In R. E. Goodin (Ed.), *The Oxford handbook of political science* (pp. 681–697). Oxford University Press.

Mayr, A., & Machin, D. (2012). *The language of crime and deviance*. Bloomsbury.

Melinkoff, D. (1963). *The language of Law*. Little, Brown & Co.

Rabuy, B., & Kopf, D. (2016). *Detaining the Poor: How money bail perpetuates an endless cycle of poverty and jail time*. https://www.prisonpolicy.org/reports/incomejails.html

Rayner, G., Barling, D., & Lang, T. (2008). Sustainable food systems in Europe: Policies, realities and futures. *Journal of Hunger & Environmental Nutrition*, *3*(2/3), 145–168. https://doi.org/10.1080/19320240802243209

Sandefur, R. L. (2008). Access to civil justice and race, class, and gender inequality. *Annual Review of Sociology*, *34*(1), 339–358. https://doi.org/10.1146/annurev.soc.34.040507.134534

Seron, C., & Munger, F. (1996). Law and inequality: Race, gender … and, of course, class. *Annual Review of Sociology*, *22*(1), 187–212. https://doi.org/10.1146/annurev.soc.22.1.187

Siapera, E., & Viejo-Otero, P. (2021). Governing hate: Facebook and digital racism. *Television & New Media*, *22*(2), 112–130. https://doi.org/10.1177/1527476420982232

Slaughter, A. (2000). A liberal theory of international law. *Proceedings of the ASIL Annual Meeting*, *94*, 240–249. https://doi.org/10.1017/S0272503700055919

Solan, L., & Tiersma, P. (2004). Author identification in American courts. *Applied Linguistics*, *25*(4), 448–465. https://doi.org/10.1093/applin/25.4.448

Turkel, G. (1990). Michel Foucault: Law, Power, and Knowledge. *Journal of Law and Society 17*(2): 170–193.

Van Dijk, T. (1998). *Ideology*. Sage.

Van Eijk, G. (2017). Socioeconomic marginality in sentencing: The built-in bias in risk assessment tools and the reproduction of social inequality. *Punishment & Society*, *19*(4), 463–481. https://doi.org/10.1177/1462474516666282

von Oelreich, J., & Milestad, R. (2017). Sustainability transformations in the balance: Exploring Swedish initiatives challenging the corporate food regime. *European Planning Studies*, *25*(7), 1129–1114. https://ideas.repec.org/a/taf/eurpls/v25y2017i7p1129-1146.html. https://doi.org/10.1080/09654313.2016.1270908

Western, B., & Muller, C. (2013). Mass incarceration, macrosociology, and the poor. *The Annals of the American Academy of Political and Social Science*, *647*(1), 166–189. https://doi.org/10.1177/0002716213475421

Protecting 'Competition, not Competitors': Antitrust discourse and the AT&T-Time Warner merger

Pawel Popiel

ABSTRACT
A key discourse underpinning US antitrust law is that it protects competition, not competitors. However, what this means in practice both has changed over time and betrays the politics underlying antitrust enforcement. This article interrogates this discourse and its contradictions in the context of the AT&T-Time Warner merger lawsuit through a critical discourse analysis of legal documents related to the case. The case represents a conflict over incentivizing competition in digital advertising markets at the expense of competition, particularly smaller competitors, in video markets. The analysis reveals how the discourse obscures the strategic choices made by courts to protect incumbent companies: by approving the merger, the court circumscribed the video programming and distribution market for consolidation to strengthen the competitive position of the merging parties in the digital advertising market dominated by Facebook and Google. Thus, this discourse masks not just the deference to dominant merging companies, but also the role of courts in shaping market competition at their behest.

Introduction

Antitrust, or competition law, exists to address potential abuses by market actors that harm market competition, which is considered essential to benefits ranging from innovation to dispersing private power. A central discourse often taken for granted in American legal rhetoric underpins this goal, namely that antitrust law protects competition, not competitors. However, what protecting competition over competitors means in practice has changed over time, and the discourse not only obscures the neoliberal politics underlying antitrust enforcement, but is also frequently invoked to justify legal approval of massive mergers. Its contradictions become especially apparent in media, telecom, and digital platform markets, which both consolidate and tend toward concentration due to network effects and economies of scale.

This article interrogates the discourse of protecting competition over competitors and its contradictions through the lens of the AT&T-Time Warner merger. Announced in 2016, the merger was challenged in court by the U.S. Department of Justice (DOJ), which pursues antitrust cases, resulting in the first vertical merger trial since the 1980s breakup of AT&T. The case became a legal referendum on vertical media mergers and on the ability of existing antitrust enforcement to address sweeping changes within digital video and advertising markets. I analyze legal documents related to this antitrust case, tracing how the discourse of protecting competition over competitors – a central tenet of U.S. antitrust enforcement – conceals the strategic choices made by courts to protect incumbents, namely the dominant merging parties, from competition, illuminating the neoliberal politics of antitrust enforcement in digital media markets. Specifically, the case represents a conflict over incentivizing competition in digital advertising markets at the expense of competition, particularly smaller competitors, in video markets. By approving the merger, the court circumscribed a market – video programming and distribution – for consolidation and attendant anticompetitive harms to strengthen the competitive position of the merging parties in the digital advertising market dominated by Facebook and Google. Though contested by the merger's opponents, the discourse masks how this deliberate court decision shapes market competition to benefit incumbents.

I begin by briefly outlining the historical context around the discourse of protecting competition over competitors in antitrust law. Next, I review the changing dynamics in converging video markets to contextualize the merger and the concerns it raised. I outline my methodological approach and then examine the legal proceedings from the court case and its subsequent appeal. I conclude by considering how the discourse of protecting competition over competitors obscures the active role of existing antitrust law in managing competition in digital media markets.

Protecting 'competition, not competitors'

Competition – the mechanism by which markets are said to self-regulate – is elusive under capitalism, since 'capital must always seek to thwart competition' (Wood, 2003, p. 22). For example, such elusiveness characterizes telecom and digital platform markets, where network effects, massive sunk costs, and economies of scale drive market concentration. Consequently, competition 'does not exist abstractly, but is influenced by the existing legal and informal institutions' (Stucke, 2013, p. 162), including courts and regulatory agencies. Yet, competition law itself 'is a social construct … embedded in society's evolving norms' (Ezrachi, 2017, p. 51), and 'based on particular discourses' (Buch-Hansen & Wigger, 2011, p. 17), which reflect ideological notions about the role of law in overseeing private markets. Since supposedly self-correcting markets require government intervention, competition policy decisions are inherently political because they 'are *always* distributive decisions' (Grewal & Purdy, 2014, p. 18, emphasis in original). Particular discourses obscure this politics, which reflects tensions within competition policy, like conceptualizing competition as freedom from government interference over competition as freedom from market power (Peritz, 2000).

The discourse of 'the protection of *competition*, not *competitors*' [emphasis in original], as the Supreme Court opined in *Brunswick Corp. v. Pueblo Bowl-O-Mat, Inc.* (1977), emphasizes a key distinction essential to antitrust enforcement. As the DOJ wrote in a 2008 report: 'Competition produces injuries; an enterprising firm may negatively affect rivals' profits or drive them out of business. But competition also benefits consumers by spurring price reductions, better quality, and innovation' (DOJ, 2008, p. 11). Thus, harming competitors does not necessarily violate antitrust law. Frequently cited in antitrust court rulings, the emphasis on protecting competition over competitors represents a guiding enforcement principle (Fox, 2003).

However, what protecting competition over competitors means in practice, like the notion of 'competitive' markets itself, has changed over time, reflecting the politics underlying antitrust law and its enforcement. The legal roots of this discourse lie in the famously liberal Warren Court of the 1950s and 1960s,[1] which defined competitive markets as comprising many competitors, with small businesses having a 'right' to compete with bigger firms (Hovenkamp, 2005). In the Supreme Court case *Brown Shoe Co. v. United States* (1962), the Court argued that while antitrust law protects competition over competitors, 'we cannot fail to recognize Congress' desire to promote competition through the protection of viable, small, locally owned business [which may result in] occasional higher costs and prices' (p. 345). The opinion embraces a robust notion of competition that includes protecting smaller competitors to prevent concentration.

Yet, in the 1970s, as part of a broader neoliberal shift, competition became detached from its liberal origins as a counterpoint to monopoly and attendant concentration of economic power. Legal and economic scholars associated with the neoliberal Chicago School, like Robert Bork, reconceptualized competition as 'competitiveness', namely the *potential* for competition (Davies, 2014), and redefined competitive markets 'in the economic coin of low prices, high output, and maximum room for innovation' (Hovenkamp, 2005, p. 2), or the 'consumer welfare' standard. With price effects as the key metric and potential rather than actual competition as a goal, the scope of what constitutes noncompetitive markets narrowed, divorcing 'the definition of "competition" from an analysis of [market] structure' (Khan, 2017, p. 972).

This shift impacted enforcement. Chicago School theorists largely saw antitrust intervention as governmental overreach into self-correcting markets (Hovenkamp, 2005). By reorienting competition as a process for reducing prices, the discourse came to justify barriers to entry and market concentration. William Kolasky, a former DOJ antitrust regulator, distills this discourse:

> [A] market is perfectly competitive when firms price their output at marginal cost [which can happen] even where there are entry barriers, with as few as two competitors ... [A]ntitrust intervention to preserve or create a larger number of rivals would harm consumer welfare'. (Kolasky, 2002, para. 6–7)

By devaluing actual competition in markets, the discourse strategically limited the circumstances in which antitrust intervention is justified: 'Competition is fiercest when competitors have no protection from their government ... The antitrust laws should intervene only when one combatant employs methods that would deny victory to the most efficient firm' (Kolasky, 2002, para. 9–11). The discourse naturalizes antitrust restraint in deference to market mechanisms, narrowing the rationale for intervention to situations in which a competitor threatens processes that drive prices to their efficient levels, often limited to horizontal integration (i.e. when two competitors merge). This antitrust paradigm is especially permissive toward vertical integration (e.g. a distributor merging with a supplier), viewing it as unproblematic (Khan, 2017). This discourse and attendant antitrust practices have implications for governing digital media markets, which I explore through the AT&T-Time Warner merger.

Competition in media markets

The tensions within the competition discourse emerge in the oversight of media markets, which are 'increasingly marked by network convergence and populated by telecom, cable and technology platforms' (Evens & Donders, 2018, p. 220), presenting challenges for regulators in maintaining competition. Vertical and horizontal integration in these markets – including of media production, distribution infrastructure, and streaming platform – is accelerated by the emergence of over-the-top (OTT) platforms like Netflix offering subscription-based digital content access 'as the dominant infrastructural and/or economic model' (Evens & Donders, 2018, p. 1). OTTs' growing popularity has accelerated cord-cutting, namely canceling pay-TV subscriptions. To compete with OTTs, dominant Internet Service Providers (ISPs) vertically integrate with media companies, pursuing control over media production and distribution to realize significant efficiencies and offer consumers bundled internet and TV (Evens & Donders, 2018; Meese, 2019). However, this consolidation facilitates the acquisition of significant market power over production and supply chains. A key challenge facing antitrust authorities in media markets involves preventing anticompetitive behavior by these vertical combinations that harms competitors or consumers, or thwarts innovation (Evens & Donders, 2018). Yet, as Just (2009) notes, media mergers are challenging to adjudicate. For instance, antitrust merger review requires careful definition of the relevant markets affected by a merger, traditionally based on product substitutability. However, technological convergence in media and telecommunications markets increasingly complicates clear distinctions between substitutable products and, by extension, market definition.

The AT&T-Time Warner merger, announced in October 2016, illustrates these developments. By acquiring Time Warner, one of the largest U.S. media companies with popular content properties like HBO, AT&T planned to significantly grow its content ownership. Yet the merger faced significant criticism from advocacy groups, policy experts, and smaller competitors. Since its 1984 breakup, AT&T has re-acquired the bulk of the companies it was forced to divest, becoming the largest U.S. wireless telecommunications and satellite pay-TV company and surpassing its own size at the time of the breakup (Smith, 2017). Critics were concerned that the merger would create incentives to thwart competition in content production and distribution markets, especially by charging above-market rates for distributing Time Warner's programming to smaller competitors, and hurt emerging OTT competitors (Steinbaum & Hwang, 2017). Moreover, the $40 billion debt incurred through the transaction along with the inclusion of premium Time Warner content in cable subscriptions signaled consumer price hikes (Picker, 2016). Despite these concerns, many commentators expected the merger to pass antitrust review given regulators' tolerance of vertical integration. Instead, the proposed acquisition faced the first vertical merger lawsuit since AT&T's break-up. An analysis of the legal arguments during the merger court case, brought by the DOJ, reveals how neoliberal interpretations of antitrust law invoke the discourse of protecting competition over competitors to legitimate consolidation in legally circumscribed media markets.

Methodology

This case study traces the discourse of protecting competition over competitors in legal documents related to the AT&T-Time Warner merger case and its appeal. The trial documents I examine (*n* = 23) include the defendants' pre-trial brief and their subsequent appeal, the DOJ's initial complaint and reply to the appeal, both court decisions, and amicus briefs, namely supplemental information submitted to courts by third parties not involved in the case, but with relevant expertise. I include amicus briefs because courts often rely on them 'for the economic reasoning justifying antitrust rules' (Khan, 2020, p. 1679), since judges may lack expertise in evaluating certain complex economic arguments.

I examine these documents using critical discourse analysis (CDA) within an interpretive critical policy framework (Fairclough, 2013; Fischer, 2003). Discourse here denotes 'language-in-use [namely] specific patterns of interaction via symbolic means' (Streeter, 2013, p. 489), emerging from institutions and power structures. While discourse is shaped by the 'ideologies, hegemonies and asymmetrical power distribution' (Ali, 2019, p. 405) that characterize these structures, it also contributes to their production and maintenance. Thus, in policy contexts, discourses not only legitimate power relations embedded in laws, policies, and policymaking processes, but also reinforce them (Streeter, 2013). Consequently, CDA also interrogates the relations between discourses and power, ideology, and state institutions (Fairclough, 2013), and the power dynamics that characterize these relations (Ali, 2019). In policy contexts, CDA 'denaturalizes the policymaking process, underscoring the belief that policy, like language itself, is a discursive construction' (Ali, 2019, p. 403), including antitrust law.

Following other critical policy scholars, this study approaches discourse 'in terms of its content, as a set of policy ideas and values, and … usage, as a process of interaction focused on policy formulation … set in institutional context' (Schmidt & Radaelli, 2004, p. 184), namely the U.S. judicial system interpreting competition law here. In critical policy studies, CDA focuses on how policy problems and solutions to them are constructed in the context of reproducing hegemony (Fairclough, 2013). Accordingly, my analysis examines how the goal of protecting competition over competitors is discursively constructed and negotiated throughout the case. Using the qualitative content analysis software *Atlas.ti*, I coded the data inductively, attuned to how the legal parties defined competition; where they located it; and how they invoked it vis-à-vis both antitrust intervention (e.g. stopping the merger) and the merging parties' competitors. To assess how power manifests in legal debates over protecting competition, I also examined the definitions and arguments the court enshrined in its legal decision and the justifications it provided, situating them in the neoliberal Chicago School framework that characterizes U.S. antitrust jurisprudence.

The AT&T-Time Warner merger case

AT&T and Time Warner pitched their merger to regulators as an innovative combination, bringing competition to the emerging video streaming market where OTTs like Netflix have become established players. They argued that any antitrust scrutiny would have to account for intense competition from OTTs and, increasingly, from ad-supported platforms like YouTube and Facebook run by tech giants. Critics stressed the merger would stifle this competition, which drove prices down and freed consumers from increasingly expensive pay-TV bundles, and pressure other giants like Verizon and twenty-first Century Fox to vertically integrate to strengthen traditional Multichannel Video

Programming Distributors' (MVPDs) dominant position against emerging digital content platforms.

Thus, the merger presented a stark choice between allowing consolidation for bigger players to compete among one other – protecting incumbent competitors – and ensuring smaller players can enter the market. As Gene Kimmelman of the advocacy organization Public Knowledge stated, 'at some point the government must take steps to promote competition and put a stop to a consolidation arms race' (Kimmelman, 2016, p. 11). By emphasizing the merger's impact on future market structure, such arguments contested the discourse of protecting competition over competitors and its defense of narrow antitrust review on the grounds that it could destroy nascent competition in these markets by normalizing consolidation as a competitive strategy among dominant media companies.

On November 20, 2017, the DOJ filed a lawsuit against the merger, citing likely price increases in cable and satellite subscriptions and anticompetitive effects on OTT platforms. These harms, the government argued, were compounded by AT&T's reach (U.S. v. AT&T, 2018d). David McAtee, AT&T's General Counsel, responded that the lawsuit represented 'a radical and inexplicable departure from decades of antitrust precedent' (Kang & de la Merced, 2017, para. 38). As Judge Leon, who presided over the case, wrote in his ruling, 'If there ever were an antitrust case where the parties had a dramatically different assessment of the current state of the relevant market and a fundamentally different vision of its future development, this is the one' U.S. v. AT&T, No. 1:17-cv-02511 (D.C. Cir. 2018).

Harming competition

The merger's opponents sought to challenge the narrow competition discourse in their legal arguments. The government argued the merger would harm competition in the video distribution market by increasing competitors' costs to Time Warner's valuable programming content. Before the merger, Time Warner would lose distribution if it charged distributors above market rates for its content. However, post-merger, AT&T would have the incentive to raise prices on and withhold Time Warner content from competing distributors to gain a significant number of competitors' subscribers, since switching to AT&T would be the only way they could now access it (U.S. v. AT&T, 2018g). This foreclosure would effectively stifle competition from emerging OTTs, which needed to expand their subscriber base to survive in the market (U.S. v. AT&T, 2018d). Similarly, competitors' amicus briefs argued that since MVPDs would lose subscribers if they lost attractive content, the merger would hurt smaller networks unable to afford the post-merger carriage fees (U.S. v. AT&T, 2018b, 2018c).

Although these arguments noted price effects, they discursively constructed threats to competition as rooted in market structure and process, in opposition to the neoliberal competition discourse exclusively focused on output. Indeed, the DOJ's case contested the Chicago School notion that vertical integration poses no competitive harms, highlighting how a vertically integrated entity would drastically alter the competitive processes within the video market, particularly for emerging OTT platform competitors. Given the legal permissiveness toward vertical mergers, part of the government's challenge rested in persuading the court the merger posed antitrust concerns falling within the bounds of the Clayton Act, which outlaws anti-competitive mergers. To make the case that the merger violated the Act, the DOJ invoked the discourse of robust pre-Chicago School competition in the landmark Warren Era antitrust case, *United States v. Philadelphia Nat'l Bank* (1963) – a strong, interventionist interpretation of antitrust law – arguing that the Clayton Act meant to protect small businesses, thwart concentration, and prevent anticompetitive practices (U.S. v. AT&T, 2018g).

Decrying the merging parties' rationale that the merger would allow them to compete with tech giants, supporting amici contested the dominant discourse which equated protecting competition with antitrust restraint. They argued the merger would facilitate competition for the merging parties at the expense of competition for smaller media companies and that such foreclosure on competition in 'one sector of the economy because [some] believe that [it] might promote greater competition in a more important sector of the economy' (U.S. v. AT&T, 2018a, p. 17) violated the spirit of antitrust. They stressed that, by allowing the merger, the court would privilege a large competitor over smaller ones, protecting a competitor over competition.

Protecting competition

The defendants deployed the narrow competition discourse by stressing the merger's potential efficiencies, while equating opponents' concerns about harms to competition with calls for legal intervention to protect competitors. They framed the merger as a legitimate response to competition from OTTs and digital platforms, which irreversibly changed the TV landscape. Since Time Warner lacked basic consumer data it could not compete with platforms like Google and Facebook to attract advertising to subsidize its subscription fees and content production costs, aggravated by cord-cutting. AT&T's rich troves of user data from its satellite TV and internet services would enable Time Warner to do so, while its distribution channels would provide the company with direct consumer access. Like digital platforms, the media giant would be able to deliver content to users without an intermediary and costly negotiations for distribution deals. Meanwhile, for AT&T acquiring content and experimenting with mobile video delivery would drive adoption of its wireless services: 'the future of video lies in its wireless network, and the future of its wireless network lies in video' (U.S. v. AT&T, 2018f, p. 21). By combining distribution infrastructure, video, and data, the defendants argued, the merger represented the 'industry's only foreseeable opportunity to create a video advertising platform with scale adequate to give advertisers a viable alternative to the duopoly of Google and Facebook' (U.S. v. AT&T, 2018f, p. 24).

These *potential* efficiencies and future competition in changing video markets conformed to the promise of market-driven innovation within the dominant competition discourse, while discursively downplaying the normalization of vertical integration in programming and distribution that opponents feared. Yet, the defendants' arguments ignored the fact that digital platforms' access to consumers was not entirely direct – they owned no distribution infrastructure, like AT&T with its national wireless network. By claiming Time Warner lacked such access, they downplayed Time Warner's successful experiment with HBO Go, an OTT platform service that offers consumers a subscription to HBO's premium content without a cable subscription. By positioning vertical integration between programming and distribution as the only alternative to a duopoly in digital advertising, they implicitly wrote off antitrust intervention in and regulation of digital advertising.

In making their case, the defendants invoked the discourse about antitrust 'protect[ing] *competition*, not competitors' (U.S. v. AT&T, 2018f, p. 6, emphasis in original), strategically diverting focus from potential harms to competitors. They addressed the alleged threats to competition by separating competition from competitors that constitute it: '[d]ispleasing [a TV network] is not the same thing as substantially lessening competition marketwide' (U.S. v. AT&T, 2018e, p. 20). They argued the government's case sought to protect certain competitors over others 'by keeping traditional [content] providers restricted to traditional models while [digital platforms like Facebook] drive innovation' (U.S. v. AT&T, 2018e, p. 6). Thus, blocking the merger would rob digital platforms and other MVPDs of competition. Moreover, they stressed that the merger would make advertising scarcer, more relevant, and more efficient, reducing consumer prices, discursively invoking the narrow, but key metric of competition in neoliberal antitrust enforcement.

Protecting competitors

On June 12, 2018, the court approved the merger, rejecting the government's arguments about anticompetitive harms, especially for emerging OTTs. In particular, the court discarded the government's centerpiece argument that withholding Time Warner content from rival distributors would benefit the merged entity's bottom line overall due to gains in competitors' subscribers. Its opinion betrays how the discourse of protecting competition over competitors masks deference to incumbent competitors in the context of media merger review. Accepting at face value the merging parties' testimony that the 'merger will increase not only innovation, but competition … for years to come' ('U.S. v. AT&T', 2018, p. 3), the opinion invokes the narrow competition discourse to justify antitrust nonintervention. By invoking the Chicago School assumption that vertical integration produces competitive "efficiencies between purchasers and sellers" ('U.S. v. AT&T', 2018, p. 57), the opinion discursively embraces the defendants' efficiency arguments, namely pairing data with advertising to create value. The court called the merger 'a vision deal' ('U.S. v. AT&T', 2018, p. 155) that will introduce 'a marketplace of data-informed advertising inventory' ('U.S. v. AT&T', 2018, p. 39) and enable experiments with personalized mobile content delivery, such as the defendants' example of creating CNN newsclips for AT&T's wireless customers. The court readily accepted that such clips represented a competitive substitute for long-form, curated OTT programming and would enable the merged entity to compete with data-driven platforms, while reducing prices for consumers.

The court opinion also discursively equates antitrust intervention with protecting competitors over competition to mask its deference to the merging parties. Framing competitors' legal objections to the merger as a competitive tactic to use the legal system against market opponents, the court rejected their testimony about the merger's anti-competitive impact on media markets, stating 'there is a threat that such testimony reflects self-interest rather than genuine concerns about harm to competition' ('U.S. v. AT&T', 2018, p. 92). Yet, the judge accepted defense witnesses' statements that the industry is the most competitive it has been in the last 30 years without factual proof. Although AT&T itself acknowledged the merger would enable it to withhold Time Warner content, the court argued that 'evidence indicating defendants' recognition that it could be possible to act in accordance with the Government's theories of harm is a far cry from evidence that the merged company is likely to do so' ('U.S. v. AT&T', 2018, p. 90). Finally, the opinion betrays the contradictory neoliberal deference to incumbents within the discourse of protecting competition over competitors by setting an accelerated timeline for concluding the case before the merger deal expires to save AT&T a $500 million breakup fee and demanding that the government not stay the merger to appeal its decision, which 'would undermine the faith in our system of justice of not only the defendants, but their millions of shareholders and the business community at large' ('U.S. v. AT&T', 2018, p. 172).

The appeal

In October 2018, the DOJ appealed the ruling, citing the court's rejection of the established economics of bargaining in programming negotiations, including Time Warner's incentives to forego profits to benefit the merged entity's bottom line. The government sought to counter the discursive pro-competitive rationale pervading the ruling by highlighting the court's defense of the merging parties in the face of competing testimony: 'The testimony of merging company executives, who stand to benefit financially from approval of a merger, deserves at least as much skepticism (if not more so) as the testimony of competitors' (U.S. v. AT&T, 2019c, pp. 59–60). Competition from OTTs challenged traditional pay-TV business models and cable bundles – by ruling in AT&T-Time Warner's favor, the court intervened in that competitive process on behalf of two incumbents threatened by that competition. Through errors, inconsistencies, and undue deference to defendant testimony, the court essentially protected competitors and not competition.

Similarly, multiple amicus briefs noted the politics pervading the court's deference to the incumbent competitors, challenging the narrow competition discourse that worked to obscure this politics, as basis for overturning the ruling. Prominent organizations like the American Antitrust Institute decried 'the court's rejection of basic economic and legal principles … [T]he court seems to have readily accepted the defendants' version of the evidence' (U.S. v. AT&T, 2019b, pp. 6–7). They argued that the court's failure to take seriously the anticompetitive dangers of vertical integration set a dangerous precedent in antitrust law: 'the district court made significant errors of economics, law, and logic [and] neither these errors nor certain extreme positions advocated by the defendants … should be enshrined into law' (U.S. v. AT&T, 2019a, p. 1). The DOJ also stressed that '[t]he outcome of this appeal will shape the future of the media and telecommunications industries for years to come' (U.S. v. AT&T, 2019c, p. 1); a testament to the durability of legal discursive constructions. The appeal represented not only an opportunity to correct a decision widely regarded as flawed, but also to forestall future vertical consolidation between content and distribution. Yet, in February 2019, the District Court of Appeals upheld the original decision, conceding that 'the district court made some problematic statements' U.S. v. AT&T, No. 18-5214 (D.C. Cir. 2019). While the merger's competitive impact remained unclear, the court found the government failed to provide sufficient evidence to support its objections to the merger and to contest the defendants' testimony.

Many advocates, policymakers, and industry members saw the merger as a blow to media competition. After the merger was consummated, contrary to the court's unwavering confidence in the defendants' testimony, AT&T raised prices on its DirecTV satellite and streaming services (Hiltzik, 2019). Moreover, as the DOJ had argued during the trial, AT&T prevented Time Warner-owned shows from streaming on rival services, including Netflix, to make its content more exclusive. AT&T's CFO John Stephens justified the $1.2 billion loss in quarterly revenue, stating that 'We made the strategic decision to give HBO Max exclusive streaming rights for top programs … In the past, we would have sold these externally' (Brodkin, 2020). Just two weeks after the initial ruling, AT&T acquired AppNexus, one of the world's largest ad exchange companies, to strengthen its competitive position in the digital advertising market dominated by Google and Facebook (Sutton, 2018). As Hernan Cristerna of JP Morgan argued, which advised AT&T on the merger, allowing consolidation served as a market-based alternative to other regulatory measures to disciplining tech giants:

> until regulators conclude that [breaking up big tech] is necessary, the United States needs an approach to merger regulation that protects consumers by supporting transactions that create enterprises capable of standing head-to-head with the tech giants. The decision to allow AT&T to acquire Time Warner is a step in this direction. (Cristerna, 2018)

Here, as in the case, the discourse of protecting competition over competitors legitimates antitrust non-intervention, deliberately fueling consolidation to offset an oligopoly in one market at the expense of competition in another. Thus, this discourse masks not just the deference to dominant merging companies, but also the role of courts in shaping market competition at their behest.

Conclusion

Although contested, the discourse of protecting competition over competitors naturalizes the narrow, pro-incumbent focus of the existing neoliberal U.S. antitrust jurisprudence. Hoisted as antitrust's primary goal, in neoliberal legal rhetoric the discourse equates antitrust intervention with skewing naturally occurring competition to protect specific competitors. Yet, as the AT&T-Time Warner case illustrates, existing antitrust enforcement makes powerful decisions about where competition can and cannot occur, often to the benefit of incumbent players, which this discourse obscures. The consumer welfare standard as a measure of market competition legitimates this logic: as long as it is *potentially* maximized – and often industry promises suffice in persuading courts – competition exists, and the market requires no intervention (Davies, 2014). In this case, the confluence of corporate interests and Chicago School influence over antitrust legal analysis protected incumbents, endangering competition in media markets.

However, rather than simply applied poorly, the case represents antitrust law applied deliberately – to contest tech giants' digital advertising oligopoly by facilitating consolidation in video markets at the expense of OTT entrants, smaller video competitors, and consumers. The AT&T-Time Warner case illuminates how the discourse of protecting competition over competitors obscures judicial intervention – greenlighting the merger and actively enshrining the rationale for it in law – to shape the boundaries of market activity. The process reveals the interventionist tendencies of neoliberal policymaking to advance the interests of dominant industry players (Davies, 2014). In this case, the court circumscribed a market, namely video programming and distribution, for consolidation and attendant potential anticompetitive harms by justifying growing, equally *potential* competition (as the appeals court itself admitted) in the digital advertising market dominated by Google and Facebook. The case, then, serves as a potent reminder that antitrust courts are involved in specifying the boundaries of market activity even when they choose not to intervene in mergers, which the narrow competition discourse conceals.

Ironically, in 2021, AT&T spun off Time Warner and other media assets to focus on telecommunications. Although some saw this as proof that the DOJ tried to prevent what market competition addressed, AT&T plans to combine Discovery with WarnerMedia, yielding another media giant. Concurrently, the U.S. government began an historic effort to revamp antitrust enforcement. The success of these reform efforts will depend partly on reformists' ability to contest the notion of competition embedded within the discourse of protecting competition over competitors.

Note

1. Named after Chief Justice Earl Warren, the Warren Court represents one of the most activist periods in U.S. Supreme Court history, including the substantial expansion of civil rights.

Disclosure statement

No potential conflict of interest was reported by the author(s).

ORCID

Pawel Popiel http://orcid.org/0000-0001-5641-581X

References

Ali, C. (2019). Analyzing talk and text III: Discourse analysis. In H. Van den Bulck, M. Puppis, K. Donders, & L. V. Audenhove (Eds.), *The Palgrave handbook of methods for media policy research* (pp. 403–418). Palgrave Macmillan.

Brodkin, J. (2020, February 4). AT&T is doing exactly what it told Congress it wouldn't do with Time Warner. *ArsTechnica*. https://arstechnica.com/information-technology/2020/02/att-lost-1-2b-by-preventing-time-warner-shows-from-airing-on-netflix/

Brown Shoe Co. v. United States, 370 U.S. 294. (1962).

Brunswick v. Pueblo Bowl-O-Mat, Inc., 429 U.S. 477. (1977).

Buch-Hansen, H., & Wigger, A. (2011). *The politics of European competition regulation: A critical political economy perspective*. Routledge.

Cristerna, H. (2018, July 3). How should antitrust regulators check Silicon Valley's ambitions? *The New York Times*. https://www.nytimes.com/2018/07/03/business/dealbook/antitrust-regulators-silicon-valley.html.

Davies, W. (2014). *The limits of neoliberalism: Authority, sovereignty and the logic of competition*. Sage.

DOJ. (2008). *Competition and monopoly: Single-firm conduct under Section 2 of the Sherman Act*. U.S. Dep't of Justice. https://www.justice.gov/sites/default/files/atr/legacy/2008/09/12/236681_chapter1.pdf

Evens, T., & Donders, K. (2018). *Platform power and policy in transforming Television markets*. Palgrave Macmillan.

Ezrachi, A. (2017). Sponge. *Journal of Antitrust Enforcement, 5*(1), 49–75. https://doi.org/10.1093/jaenfo/jnw011

Fairclough, N. (2013). Critical discourse analysis and critical policy studies. *Critical Policy Studies, 7*(2), 177–197. https://doi.org/10.1080/19460171.2013.798239

Fischer, F. (2003). *Reframing public policy: Discursive politics and deliberative practices*. Oxford University Press.

Fox, E. M. (2003). We protect competition, you protect competitors. *World Competition, 26*(2), 149–165. https://heinonline.org/HOL/LandingPage?handle=hein.kluwer/wcl0048&div=15; https://doi.org/10.54648/WOCO2003002

Grewal, D. S., & Purdy, J. (2014). Introduction: Law and neoliberalism. *Law & Contemp. Probs., 77*(1), 1–23. https://scholarship.law.duke.edu/faculty_scholarship/3141

Hiltzik, M. (2019, March 18). AT&T raises DirecTV Now prices, making chumps of those who backed Time Warner merger. *The Los Angeles Times*. https://www.latimes.com/business/hiltzik/la-fi-hiltzik-att-price-rise-20190318-story.html.

Hovenkamp, H. (2005). *The antitrust enterprise: Principle and execution*. Harvard University Press.

Just, N. (2009). Measuring media concentration and diversity: New approaches and instruments in Europe and the US. *Media, Culture & Society, 31*(1), 97–117. https://doi.org/10.1177/0163443708098248

Kang, C., & de la Merced, M. J. (2017, November 20). Justice department sues to block AT&T-Time Warner Merger. *The New York Times*. https://www.nytimes.com/2017/11/20/business/dealbook/att-time-warner-merger.html.

Khan, L. (2017). The ideological roots of America's market power problem. *The Yale Law Journal Forum, 127*, 960–979. https://heinonline.org/HOL/LandingPage?handle=hein.journals/yljfor127&div=50.

Khan, L. (2020). The End of antitrust history revisited. *Harvard Law Review, 133*(5), 1655–1682. https://heinonline.org/HOL/LandingPage?handle=hein.journals/hlr133&div=80&id=&page=

Kimmelman, G. (2016, December 7). *Testimony of Gene Kimmelman, President & CEO, public knowledge*. Subcommittee on Antitrust, Competition Policy & Consumer Rights. https://www.judiciary.senate.gov/imo/media/doc/12-07-16%20Kimmelman%20Testimony1.pdf.

Kolasky, W. J. (2002, October 28). *What is competition?* Department of Justice. https://www.justice.gov/atr/speech/what-competition.

Meese, J. (2019). Telecommunications companies as digital broadcasters: The importance of net neutrality in competitive markets. *Television & New Media, 21*, 530–546. https://doi.org/10.1177/1527476419833560

Peritz, R. J. R. (2000). *Competition policy in America: History, rhetoric, law*. Oxford University Press.

Picker, L. (2016, October 23). *To secure a mega-merger, AT&T plans to shoulder mega-debt*. https://www.nytimes.com/2016/10/24/business/dealbook/att-plans-to-shoulder-mega-debt-merger-time-warner.html?mcubz=0.

Schmidt, V. A., & Radaelli, C. M. (2004). Policy change and discourse in Europe: Conceptual and methodological issues. *West European Politics, 27*(2), 183–210. https://doi.org/10.1080/0140238042000214874

Smith, A. (2017, March 21). *What's AT&T's scale and valuation?* http://marketrealist.com/2017/03/whats-atts-scale-and-valuation/.

Steinbaum, M., & Hwang, A. (2017). *Crossed lines: Why the AT&T-time Warner Merger demands a new approach to antitrust*. The Roosevelt Institute. http://rooseveltinstitute.org/wp-content/uploads/2017/02/CrossedLines_Feb17_v2.pdf.

Streeter, T. (2013). Policy, politics, and discourse. *Communication, Culture & Critique, 6*(4), 488–501. https://doi.org/10.1111/cccr.12028

Stucke, M. E. (2013). Is competition always good? *Journal of Antitrust Enforcement, 1*(1), 162–197. https://doi.org/10.1093/jaenfo/jns008

Sutton, K. (2018, June 25). What AT&T's acquisition of AppNexus means. *Adweek.* https://www.adweek.com/digital/what-atts-acquisition-of-appnexus-means/

U.S. v. AT&T. (2018a). *AMICUS CURIAE* BRIEF OF JOSEPH M. ALIOTO IN SUPPORT OF THE UNITED STATES OF AMERICA FOR AN ORDER ENJOINING THE PROPOSED ACQUISITION. D.C. Cir. (no. 1:17-cv-02511). https://www.courtlistener.com/recap/gov.uscourts.dcd.191339/gov.uscourts.dcd.191339.144.0.pdf

U.S. v. AT&T. (2018b). *BRIEF OF CINÉMOI NORTH AMERICA AS AMICUS CURIAE IN SUPPORT OF THE UNITED STATES OF AMERICA.* D.C. Cir. (no. 1:17-cv-02511). https://www.courtlistener.com/recap/gov.uscourts.dcd.191339/gov.uscourts.dcd.191339.135.1.pdf

U.S. v. AT&T. (2018c). BRIEF OF RCN TELECOM SERVICES, LLC, GRANDE COMMUNICATIONS NETWORKS, LLC, AND WAVEDIVISION HOLDINGS, LLC, AND AMERICAN CABLE ASSOCIATION AS AMICI CURIAE IN SUPPORT OF NEITHER PARTY. D.C. Cir. (no. 1:17-cv-02511). https://acaconnects.org/brief-w-rcn-grande-and-wave-broadband-as-amici-curiae-in-support-of-neither-party-re-u-s-v-att-inc/

U.S. v. AT&T. (2018d). *COMPLAINT.* D.C. Cir. (no. 1:17-cv-02511). https://www.courtlistener.com/recap/gov.uscourts.dcd.191339/gov.uscourts.dcd.191339.1.0_2.pdf

U.S. v. AT&T. (2018e). POST-TRIAL BRIEF OF DEFENDANTS AT&T INC., DIRECTV GROUP HOLDINGS, LLC, AND TIME WARNER INC. D.C. Cir. (no. 1:17-cv-02511)

U.S. v. AT&T. (2018f). *PRETRIAL BRIEF OF DEFENDANTS AT&T INC., DIRECTV GROUP HOLDINGS, LLC, AND TIME WARNER INC.* D.C. Cir. (no. 1:17-cv-02511). https://www.courtlistener.com/recap/gov.uscourts.dcd.191339/gov.uscourts.dcd.191339.77.0_1.pdf

U.S. v. AT&T. (2018g). *PROPOSED CONCLUSIONS OF LAW OF THE UNITED STATES.* D.C. Cir. (no. 1:17-cv-02511). https://www.courtlistener.com/recap/gov.uscourts.dcd.191339/gov.uscourts.dcd.191339.127.0_1.pdf

U.S. v. AT&T. (2019a). *BRIEF FOR 27 ANTITRUST SCHOLARS AS AMICI CURIAEIN SUPPORT OF NEITHER PARTY* D.C. Cir. (no. 18-5214). https://www.docketbird.com/court-documents/USA-v-AT-T-Inc-et-al/AMICUS-FOR-APPELLANT-FINAL-BRIEF-1755903-filed-by-Jonathan-B-Baker-Michael-A-Carrier-William-S-Comanor-Aaron-Edlin-Einer-R-Elhauge-Harry-First-Eleanor-M-Fox-Martin-Gaynor-Joseph-Harrington-Herbert-Hovenkamp-James-Kearl-Robert-Lande-Marina-L-Lao-Marga/cadc-2018-05214-01208070971

U.S. v. AT&T. (2019b). *BRIEF OF AMICI CURIAE AMERICAN ANTITRUST INSTITUTE, CONSUMERS UNION, AND PUBLIC KNOWLEDGE IN SUPPORT OF APPELLANT.* D.C. Cir. (no. 18-5214). https://www.antitrustinstitute.org/wp-content/uploads/2018/08/AAI-USATT-Amicus-1.pdf

U.S. v. AT&T. (2019c). *FINAL, CORRECTED BRIEF OF APPELLANT UNITED STATES OF AMERICA.* D.C. Cir. (no. 18-5214). https://www.justice.gov/atr/case-document/file/1085516/download

U.S. v. AT&T, No. 18-5214 (D.C. Cir.) (2019).

U.S. v. AT&T, No. 1:17-cv-02511 (D.C. Cir.) (2018).

Wood, E. M. (2003). *Empire of capital.* Verso.

Applying the principles of *Vivir Bien* to a court resolution in Bolivia: language, discourse, and land law

María Itatí Dolhare and Sol Rojas-Lizana

ABSTRACT
The Plurinational Constitutional Court is the final arbiter of legal disputes involving the interpretation and application of the *Political Constitution of the Plurinational State of* Bolivia (2009) (BC). Its role is especially important given that the BC follows a type of decolonial 'hybrid' constitutional model that incorporates the Indigenous concept of *Vivir Bien (VB)* as part of their legal paradigm. Using tools from Case Law Analysis and Critical Discourse Analysis, this article explores the Court's judicial interpretation and application of *VB* and its principles to a legal dispute regarding Indigenous Peoples' constitutional right to be consulted over government measures impacting their ancestral territories. The results indicate that the judges would foreground and background different aspects of the *VB* principles to support their views, resorting to their use in a hierarchical form that is not mandated in the BC. This shows a gap between formal incorporation and the practical application of the *VB* principles. This research informs the fields of legal studies, decolonial thought, and discourse studies.

Introduction

Contemporary modern liberal constitutions in the Western and Westernised world (Grosfoguel, 2013) are typically informed by dominant Western epistemologies. Modern liberal constitutionalism can be explained as 'a set of formal legal and political concepts [that consist of] the division and limitation of governmental power, the recognition and protection of certain individual rights, the protection of private property, and the notion of representative or democratic government' (ButleRitchie, 2004, p. 6).

Following its independence from Spain in the nineteenth century, the newly formed Bolivian republic adopted a succession of modern liberal constitutions mirroring European constitutional discourses. This practice continued uninterrupted until the enactment in 2009 of the Bolivian Constitution discussed here. The BC is a type of decolonial 'hybrid' model that incorporates the Indigenous-based communitarian paradigm of *Vivir Bien* (*VB*) on its legal framework. The Bolivian Plurinational Constitutional Court (PCC) is the constitutionally appointed final arbiter of legal disputes involving the interpretation and application of the principles found in the BC. This article explores the PCC's interpretation and application of *VB* and its principles to the resolution of a legal dispute regarding Indigenous Peoples' constitutional right to be consulted over government measures affecting their ancestral territories.[1] Using Case Law Analysis to find, classify and thematize the data, and complementing it with tools from Critical Discourse Analysis (e.g. discursive strategies, intensifiers, hedges, framing, perspective), the study shows that the judges would foreground and background different *VB* principles to support their view of the conflict, resorting to their use in a hierarchical form that is not mandated in the BC.

In this article we start by giving a brief background to the BC and the paradigm of *VB*. We then describe and contextualise our data and methodology. Finally, two of *VB*'s principles are used to analyse the different judicial views deployed in the judgment.

The Bolivian constitution and *Vivir Bien*

The constitution of a country is its fundamental law. The principles and institutions incorporated in it shape and guide the nation-state. Modern liberal constitutions, initially embodied emancipatory legal projects favouring the 'white' European male bourgeoisie. In the former colonies, they provided a legal background for the newly independent countries. Often, they advanced and protected the views embraced by its elite minorities – usually descendants from European settlers (Clavero, 2010). Furthermore, one of the central criticisms aimed at modern liberal constitutions in Latin America is their top-down origin and their failure to adequately represent excluded groups, such as Indigenous Peoples and Afro-descendants (Viciano Pastor & Martínez Dalmau, 2010).

Vivir Bien is a Spanish extrapolation of the ancient concept of *Suma Qamaña* which has been translated into English as Living Well (Together), Good Life or Life in Plenitude (Teixeira Delgado, 2018). It re-emerged strongly in the political arena around the last decade of the twentieth century and the early years of the twenty-first century (Acosta, 2013; Caudillo Félix, 2012; Chivi Vargas, 2010), as an indigenous political proposal during the Bolivian 2002 elections (Chivi Vargas, 2010). *Suma Qamaña* called for a highly equalitarian democracy, with equal opportunities and redistribution of wealth in favour of underrepresented Bolivians. *VB* is based in Andean cosmovisions and can be defined as:

> A communitarian paradigm that represents a culture of life, seeking to live well by adopting ways of life and ethical principles that interact in a respectful, harmonious, and balanced way with all living things and that are based upon the idea that everything is interconnected, interdependent and interrelated. (Huanacuni Mamani, 2010, p. 11)

The constitutional incorporation of *VB* seeks to revalorise non-Eurocentric thinking as a means of pursuing a more socially inclusive and environmentally responsible society. The BC incorporates with equal legal rank, principles rooted in modern liberal legal tradition and principles derived from *VB* as a decolonising legal project. Thus, the BC embodies a novel constitutional project in which, these two forms of knowledge engage 'in order to design and carry out counterhegemonic, intercultural uses of such a conceptions or instruments' (De Sousa Santos, 2014, p. 239). Dolhare (2019) has identified a set of four constitutional principles created to materialise *VB* and assist with its implementation as the overarching constitutional aim. These are *the plurinational and communitarian state, pluralism, interculturality, and alternative to development.* [2] They are legal tools that further the role of *VB*, into a decolonising legal project. Two of these principles will be described below as their understanding and judicial application are essential to this paper's argument.

This first principle is the concept of *plurinational and communitarian state*. Article 1 of the Constitution describes the Bolivian state as *plurinational and communitarian*. Thus, within the broader structure of Bolivia as a single nation, the plurality of indigenous cosmovisions[3] (that is, worldviews and epistemologies) is incorporated based on their cultural identity which is diverse rather than monocultural. Furthermore, the material implementation of this plurinational and communitarian state cannot be achieved unless the rights of indigenous nations and peoples that have, historically conformed the 'invisible' other side of the abyssal line (de Sousa Santos, 2014) are expressly incorporated and protected in the Constitution.

The second principle, *pluralism*, is the logical consequence of plurality (the co-existence of more than one social or homogenous social group), and is reflected in the variety of political, economic, legal, cultural, and linguistic forms adopted by this plurality of social groups. This plurality of nations and communities implies the reformulation of the modern liberal notion of one nation and one culture.

Data

The data was sourced from the Plurinational Constitutional Judgment 0300/2012, in which the PCC was asked to determine the content and scope of Indigenous Peoples' constitutional right to be consulted about legislation authorising the construction of a highway across the Indigenous Protected Area and National Park *Isiboro Sécure* (TIPNIS by its Spanish initials). In the judicial decision analysed, the PCC determined the constitutional validity of some of the legislative provisions.

The contested Act 222 provided for the Indigenous Peoples inhabiting the TIPNIS to be consulted regarding the construction of a highway across the TIPNIS. In issuing its decision, the Court must interpret and apply *VB* and its set of constitutional principles to assess whether the legislative provisions are constitutionally valid.

Method

The method to analyse the data was Case Law Analysis (CLA). As Hall and Wright (2008, p. 64) explain, this method of legal analysis involves 'reading a collection of cases, finding common threads in the legal reasoning and opinions, and commenting on their significance'. The purpose is to study different legal issues to ascertain how the courts developed principles and rules to resolve them. CLA is complemented with tools from Critical Discourse Analysis (CDA). This combination allows for more detailed attention to language and its emergent meanings, given that CDA focuses on what is being said and how it is presented, as form and content contribute to the construction of meaning in discourse (Rojas-Lizana, 2019).

More specifically, we follow the categories of analysis proposed by Reisigl and Wodak (2001), in which after identifying the corpus and topics (using CLA), we explore the discursive strategies and linguistic means employed to support the judicial arguments. In examining these linguistic elements, we examined intensifying and mitigation strategies, framing, foregrounding/backgrounding, and perspective (Lee, 2001; Rojas-Lizana, 2019). These strategies and linguistic means are emphasised in bold when presenting examples to illustrate the analysis.

CDA assumes that language is 'constitutive', as it creates and changes meaning, and that discourse needs to be understood in its situated context; in this case, the hybrid BC, the language of law and its performative power, which becomes especially forceful in the case of a constitutional judgment. This is because, the BC provides that the decisions of the PCC are binding and of obligatory compliance. As the highest court in Bolivia, no subsequent ordinary appeal of its decisions is allowed.[4]

Analysis: the Court's interpretation of the constitutional principles of *Vivir Bien*

This analysis examines the PCC's judicial interpretation and application of two constitutional principles of *VB* in a specific legal dispute called Plurinational Constitutional Judgment 0300/2012 (handed down by the PCC on 18 June 2012). In this legal dispute, the PCC was called to decide if certain legislative provisions incorporated in Act 222 were inconsistent with some constitutional principles. If that was the case, then the supremacy of the constitutional principles over the contravening provisions needed to be upheld by the PCC.

The contravening provisions were incorporated in Act 222. Act 222 allowed for the development of the TIPNIS but stipulated that Indigenous Peoples should be consulted as to the government decision to build a highway across their ancestral lands. The central legal matters raised by the allegedly contravening provisions of Act 222, can be described as follows:

1. confirming Indigenous Peoples have a constitutional right to prior, free, and informed consultation (right to consultation) over the construction of the highway on their ancestral territories, and,

2. if the Court were to answer the first question in the affirmative, to decide as to the scope and extent of this indigenous communitarian right in the context of the BC and international treaties.[5]

The decision of the PCC in the Plurinational Constitutional Judgment 0300/2012 was reached by a majority vote of 6 to 1.[6] The judgment was delivered in two separate documents. The 6 majority judges issued one joint *Majority Vote* (MV, 72 pages), and 1 minority judge issued a separate *Dissenting Vote* (DV, 36 pages).[7]

The majority upheld the constitutional validity of the questioned provisions in Act 222 stipulating that Indigenous Peoples should be consulted over the construction of the highway across their ancestral territories. The minority judge took a different view and found most of the questioned provisions were inconsistent with the BC and, therefore, they should be removed from the text of Act 222.

In the analysis below, we explore the way in which two principles of *VB* were interpreted by the Court.

First principle: plurinational and communitarian state

In connection with the constitutional principle of the plurinational and communitarian state, we observe that the majority vote begins its legal reasoning, remarking that article 1[8] creates a new model of state that is plurinational and communitarian, moving Bolivia away from the one nation – one culture model. This is a direct consequence of the incorporation with equal constitutional standing of communitarian indigenous rights and Western-style individual rights.[9]

The majority also mentions Indigenous Peoples' constitutional right to self-determination and autonomy within the framework of the unified Bolivian state. In doing so, this plurinational and communitarian state must allow Indigenous Peoples the exercise of their political, judicial, and legal systems in accordance with their cosmovisions.[10] Moreover, their participation in the national state' organs and institutions must be guaranteed.[11] Similarly, the minority judge says that the plurinational aspect symbolises the will to construct and participate in a common government that recognises cultural differences (DV, p. 2). However, his definition of the plurinational state foregrounds indigenous rights as a priority:

> a political, legal, territorial, and economic organisation that seeks to constitute a fair and harmonious society **cemented** upon decolonisation and the **consolidation** of the identities of **indigenous nations and peoples**. Therefore, the plurinational state adopts a non-classic structure that does not respond to the mono cultural logic of Western civilisation. Essentially, the plurinational state is sustained on the concept of pluralism or the existence of many. It **embodies** new ways to **construct** a state **based on indigenous peoples' struggles and demands**. (DV, p. 1, our emphasis)[12]

The example above shows that the dissenting judge stresses that 'indigenous nations and peoples' are the essential piece to 'cement / consolidate / construct a state' and achieve 'a fair and harmonious society'. The same judge observes, later in the document, that the plurinational state represents a new kind of political organisation (DV, p. 2) framing the coexistence of all the communities that make up the Bolivian people.[13]

The majority also notes that this plurinational state, as per the words of the Constitution's preamble, represents an historical challenge of collectively building a new model of statehood. Majority and minority judges agree that this must be achieved within the unity of the Bolivian state and without fracturing the territorial integrity of Bolivia. This plurinational state promotes the coexistence between indigenous and non-indigenous communities, in equality of conditions, and within their own practises and logics as civilisations (DV, p. 2). While the majority and the minority judge agree on this, there is a noticeable difference in their approaches. The majority adopts a more neutral and balanced discourse, discussing the plurinational aspects in a manner that resembles Western judicial decisions as evidenced by the type of discussion and language used:

> The quoted jurisprudence clearly establishes that the new constitutional order has as its purpose **the collective construction of the new state**, in which **pluralism provides the central base of the new judicial, political, and social structure** and whereby **individual and collective rights** must be protected by the state as well as creating the state's duty of materialising constitutional rights in accordance with the provisions of the BC. (MV, p.22, our emphasis)

If we contrast the discourse of this example with that used in the previous extract, we can see the absence of descriptors that diverge from traditional legal nomenclature due to their ambiguity within that legal frame: 'fair and harmonious', 'identity', 'embodies', 'struggles and demands.' This type of language is present in the BC, but mainly in its preamble since the genre 'constitutional preamble' allows the inclusion of non-legal discourse (Rojas-Lizana & Dolhare 2021). Interestingly, the use of legal nomenclature in the above extract from the MV also renders the reading ambiguous, as it seems too general and does not illuminate the meaning of pluralism.

The minority judge also emphasises, by stating it very early on and by repetition, that the plurinational state is a response to the colonial violence of the past and the need to decolonise the model of state as embodied by the one nation – one culture Western Modernity's notion (DV, p.1-2). *VB*'s role as a critique and alternative paradigm to the dominant paradigm of Western Modernity is clearly articulated through the whole discourse of the dissenting vote, as in this example: 'Their [indigenous peoples'] epistemologies and cosmovisions have been systematically denied by the classic liberal and colonial state but their existence is now recognised' (DV, p. 1). The mention of colonial violence is not foregrounded in the MV' discourse.

Regarding the new state's communitarian aspect, the majority and minority votes share two starting points. First is the fundamental importance of indigenous rights to the consolidation of this new Bolivian state.[14] Second, in line with the desire to preserve the country's unity, achieving *VB* requires the whole Bolivian society involvement as a community. Hence, the majority speaks of this 'collective construction of the new Bolivian state' (MV, p. 21).

Furthermore, the majority and the minority agree that the new state represents a point of departure from traditional models of Western modern liberal constitutions, as they both use clear and abundant contrastive expressions and hedgings to compare these two systems:

> The plurinational state [...] **transcends** the model of liberal and monocultural state grounded in the protection of **individual rights**. [...] This **does not** signify the denial of individual rights and guarantees. However, the **plurinational approach** to legal rights conceives them **first** as collective rights in pursuit of social interest **and second** as individual rights that must be exercised for the benefit of each community. (DV, p. 2-3, our emphasis)

This agreement is expressed in the understanding that the BC focuses on the recognition and protection of indigenous and non-indigenous communitarian rights, rather than adopting a liberal modern approach privileging individual rights. Thus, within this conception of plurinational and communitarian state, constitutional rights, duties, and guarantees cannot solely be based on the traditional modern liberal discourse because this approach enabled the continuity of the colonial difference.

In sum, the majority and the minority votes agree that the constitutional incorporation and implementation of communitarian indigenous rights constitutes a core element in the configuration of the new model of plurinational and communitarian state. However, the MV's discourse is more traditional and conciliatory. The DV on its part, emphasises indigenous rights and epistemologies as a priority, and stresses that the dominant Western model has been an impediment to achieve *VB*, for the role of this new state is to 'construct a just and harmonious society, built on decolonisation, without discrimination or exploitation, with full social justice, to strengthen the plurinational identities'.[15]

Second principle: pluralism

Regarding pluralism, recognising and adopting different knowledges, the majority judges point out that recognition of Indigenous Peoples' ancestral connection to their territories is one of international law's main criteria of its definition of Indigenous Peoples (MV, p. 30). While describing Indigenous Peoples' rights to their land and territories, the majority privileges traditional definitions sourced from international documents[16] incorporated into the constitutional text,[17] as well as the Court's prior decisions and other provisions of the BC.[18]

In the opinion of the majority, Indigenous Peoples' inherent rights to their lands and territories configure other indigenous collective rights, such as the right to be consulted. Thus, Indigenous Peoples' undisturbed exercise of their collective rights is indissolubly linked to the extent and scope of their rights over their lands and territories (MV, p. 32). The exploitation of non-renewable resources on their lands or the implementation of mega-projects are, according to the majority vote, clear examples of government activities that require the affected Indigenous Peoples to be consulted (MV, p. 35). This reasoning shows that within the principle of pluralism, the majority prefers to base their argument on the 'recognition' of difference rather than the 'adoption' of it.

On his part, the minority judge dedicates a lengthy discussion to indigenous notions of *land* and *territory* and their relevance to Indigenous Peoples to put in evidence that pluralism means not just accepting but also understanding epistemological variety. He notes that land and territory are different concepts at the heart of Indigenous Peoples' historical struggles and demands (DV, p. 8). He defines land as the physical, geographic, and vital space directly occupied by a family unit or an indigenous community and the source of their basic subsistence needs (DV, p. 8). Territory has a wider meaning as it 'is linked to their ancestry, culture, historical tradition, institutions and cosmovisions. It is an irreplaceable cultural, economic, and social space for their flourishing and survival as Indigenous Peoples' (DV, p. 8). The minority judge stresses that land and territory need to be interpreted considering Indigenous Peoples' decolonising and liberating horizon (DV, p. 8). This is because their struggles are intimately connected with their demands for emancipation, self-determination, and freedom, which are shaped by their understanding of land and territory as '*la casa común*' (the common house) for all species (DV, p. 8). This deep-rooted relationship between Indigenous Peoples and their land and territory is, according to their cosmovision, not just physical but also spiritual and deserving full legal protection. They understand their territory as:

> **alive** and embodying the **basic cell** for the existence and the advancement of their cultural identity as well as the communication of their ancestral knowledge about, and of, their community. In this sense, the **great house**, the **land without evil**, the **sacred hill** can be considered as a **living entity**. (DV, p. 9, our emphasis)

This passage shows the effort on the part of the minority judge to explain the importance of considering the central role of life within a legal system and the need to adopt an intercultural interpretation of it. The minority judge criticises Western Modernity's perception of land as a mere object to be commercialised for individual profit. He contrasts this approach with indigenous cosmovisions of land as a living entity not to be 'owned' and allowing Indigenous Peoples to procure from their land everything indispensable to ensure *VB* (DV, p. 9). From this perspective, the survival of human beings is clearly dependent on the preservation of the good health of their land and territory. In other words, Indigenous thought promotes a biocentric rather than anthropocentric discourse.

Although, the Court's majority also recognises the importance of life as life in plenitude or *VB*, their discourse about land and territory appears to prefer a Western-based approach. This is because the majority vote, concentrates their arguments on two main areas. First, they refer to international documents and the block of constitutionality as the mechanism of constitutional incorporation of international rights and obligations. Second, their vote relies on these international documents to define Indigenous Peoples' rights to their lands and territories. Thus, the position of the majority vote is clearly delimited by the international framework. The main issue with this approach is that, as Anghie and Chimni (2003) note, international law has often played an instrumental role in reproducing the colonial distinction between civilisation and barbarism, thus, justifying 'civilising missions' being deployed over these 'primitive' people and their lands and territories.

Discussion: the decision

In Plurinational Constitutional Judgment 0300/2012, the majority held, by 6 votes to 1, upheld the constitutional validity of the allegedly contravening provisions of Act 222. The Court's majority ordered the consultation process with Indigenous Peoples to proceed in accordance with the provisions of Act 222 and subject to judicial overseeing. However, the majority interpreted this right to be consulted in an extremely narrow manner with limited scope for Indigenous Peoples to deny their consent. This paper argues that the majority approach is more closely aligned with Western legal systems traditional understanding of land as an object usually owned and controlled by the 'superior and civilised subjects'.

The dissenting judge also conceded that Indigenous Peoples should be consulted about government measures affecting their ancestral land. However, he adopted a broader interpretation of the right consistent with *VB*'s biocentric discourse. Hence, for the minority judge, the right of Indigenous Peoples to be consulted should have been extended to allow them to deny their consent in accordance with their uses, customs and cosmovisions.

Overall, it can be argued that the majority's position represents a discourse more akin with Western Modernity's epistemological and legal notions, while the dissenting judge adopts a discourse more closely aligned with *VB* as representative of non-Western based epistemological and legal notions. The central consequence of these outlooks is that, while both majority and minority appear to adopt, in theory, very similar views, their material application of *VB* and its constitutional principles to the resolution of the legal issues at hand, highlights the contrast between their approaches.

At the core of the decision delivered in Plurinational Constitutional Judgement 0300/2012 is the determination of the content and scope of Indigenous Peoples' communitarian right to 'be consulted by appropriate procedures, in particular, through their institutions, each time legislative or administrative measures may be foreseen to affect them'.[19] The right to be consulted is a central element of *VB* as a decolonising process. Thus, effective implementation of this decolonising mechanism heavily hinges in the elimination of the colonial difference imposed because of the racial classification of the colonised population and their cosmovisions as inferior and uncivilised. According to Decolonial Thought, the colonial difference embodies the pervading and continuing legacy of European colonialism that still permeates the production of knowledge and the laws enacted because of it (De Sousa Santos, 2000, 2002 and 2014). It justifies considering Western-based discourses as the sole producers of universal and truthful knowledge and the discourse of Western-based legal systems, here modern liberal constitutions, as superior legal systems to be mirrored by the former colonies post-independence.

It is within this historical context of inequality and racially based naturalisation of relations of domination and oppression, that the Court was called to issue its decision. The ways the majority judges and the dissenting judge approached this task provides evidence of the relevance given to the principles of *VB* as the constitutional mechanisms of implementation of *VB* as a decolonising legal project.

Apart from what has been discussed here regarding the majority and minority discourses, it is also remarkable, that, in their decision, the majority adopts a narrow interpretation of the right to deny consent while consulted. This is because, even within a purely Western-based approach, there are broader interpretations that could have represented an advancement towards preserving a harmonious and balanced coexistence between all communities inhabiting Mother Earth as predicated by *VB*. Instead, the majority privileges a very narrow application of international law rules while deciding there are three only circumstances in which indigenous peoples can deny their consent. First, if the proposed measure may result in their displacement from their territories. Second, the storage of dangerous and harmful materials on their territories. Third, large-scale projects that may have a major impact upon their territories.

Moreover, the majority narrows these three exceptions with another test: *the less damaging alternative test*. In their opinion, even in the case of the three exceptions mentioned above, Indigenous Peoples and the government must attempt to find the less damaging options for carrying out the proposed administrative or legislative measures. Only if it is concluded that implementing this less damaging alternative places Indigenous Peoples' survival in jeopardy, then they are granted the right to deny their consent (MV, p. 41). Surprisingly, in the interpretation of the Court's majority, the proposed construction of the highway did not fall within any of the three accepted exceptions. It is unclear why the majority failed to consider the construction of a highway across a national park and protected indigenous territory a large-scale project triggering Indigenous Peoples' right to deny their consent.

The decision of the majority negatively influences the material implementation and limits the advancement of *VB* as a decolonising legal project. This is because, if Indigenous Peoples have, in the view of the majority, a very limited right to deny their consent regarding government measures affecting their territory, it follows that indigenous nations and peoples, although recognised by the BC, are not considered in the same level of the traditional Bolivian nation-state.

This subordinated place given to indigenous nations and peoples' springs from an interpretation of territory and land that is aligned with the dominant paradigm of Western Modernity's reductionist notions of territory and land instead of indigenous holistic ones. This limited understanding may be considered indicative of the failure to adopt a truly and critical intercultural approach that challenges the historical *status quo* of the colonial difference based upon a racial classification of the Bolivian population and their lands and territories as primitive, inferior and in need of 'development'.

The precedent now set by the decision in Plurinational Constitutional Judgment 0300/2012 reduces substantially the chances of advancing the principles of *VB* proposed to decolonise the constitutional text. There is no denying that this is a highly politicised matter still far from resolved, and a discussion of its intricacies falls outside the scope of this article (see Westman, 2013). Be this as it may, even though the Court's majority position is difficult to explain from a legal perspective; merely ascribing their approach to political factors, or to idiosyncratic interpretations of the BC, risks missing some of the subtler elements at play. To this end, this article makes use of tools from both CLA and CDA to examine the underlying views informing both the majority and the minority judgements. Overall, the findings of our analysis serve as a cautionary tale for future constitutional projects. This is because as evidenced here, the material implementation of constitutional principles such as *VB*, formally seeking to change the relationship between humankind and nature by fostering intercultural consensus building in highly diverse societies, may be thwarted by dominant discourses underlying the judicial interpretation and application of the same constitutional principles.

Conclusion

This article explored the ways in which two principles of *VB were* interpreted and applied by the Plurinational Constitutional Court to resolve a legal dispute. This legal dispute centred upon the content and extent of one of the fundamental constitutional rights granted to Indigenous Peoples: the right to be consulted in matters affecting their territories.

The case law analysis of the Plurinational Constitutional Judgment 0300/2012 produced the following findings: the majority and the minority of the PCC reached theoretical positions that have more commonalities than differences. Yet in terms of the practical application of *VB and* the implementation of its constitutional principles, there were some notable differences, with the majority leaning towards a more Western-based approach while the minority clearly favoured indigenous ideas, particularly regarding the meaning of land and territory. Thus, while the majority seems to stay within the limits of softer versions of Western modern liberal constitutionalism, the minority advances the notion of *VB as* a critique and alternative to the dominant paradigm of Western Modernity.

Notes

1. BC, article 196(I). Article 203 states that 'The decisions and sentences of the Pluri-National Constitutional Court are binding and of obligatory compliance, and no subsequent ordinary appeal of them is allowed.'
2. See Dolhare (2019) for a detailed explanation and exemplification of these constitutional principles. See also article 13 I-III of the BC. To find the English translation of the Constitution in the references, see: 'Bolivia, Plurinational State of. (2009).'

3. Cosmovision is defined in the Law Insider Dictionary as, 'the conception that indigenous peoples have, both collectively and individually, of the physical and spiritual world and the environment in which they conduct their lives.' https://www.lawinsider.com/dictionary/cosmovision. Accessed 7/12/2021.
4. Pursuant to section 203 of the BC.
5. For further discussions see, Anaya (2015), Lacroix (2012), and Ward (2011).
6. There are 7 judges in the PCC, and they are elected by universal suffrage. See article 199 (I) of the BC.
7. This Court resolution can be found at: https://buscador.tcpbolivia.bo/_buscador/(S(zaof3ga4uuicwimtzaptkggq))/WfrJurisprudencia1.aspx
8. Unless otherwise specified, when 'articles' are mentioned, they refer to articles in the BC.
9. BC, article 13.
10. BC, article 30 (II) (14).
11. BC, article 30 (II) (18).
12. All data has been translated from Spanish by the first author.
13. For a definition of the Bolivian people see article 3 of the BC.
14. This communitarian aspect is exemplified by article 30 of the BC, which grants communitarian rights to indigenous peoples.
15. BC, article 9 (1).
16. Convention 169 - Concerning Indigenous and Tribal Peoples in Independent Countries of the International Labour Organization (1989), articles 7, 13 and 14 and United Nations Declaration on the Rights of Indigenous Peoples (2007), article 26.
17. BC, article 410 (II).
18. The majority maintains that indigenous peoples enjoy the following rights to their lands and territories, (a) the right to the lands, territories and resources which they have traditionally owned, occupied or otherwise used or acquired; (b) the right to own, use, develop and control the lands, territories and resources that they possess by reason of traditional ownership or other traditional occupation or use, as well as those which they have otherwise acquired; (c) States shall give legal recognition and protection to these lands, territories and resources. Such recognition shall be conducted with due respect to the customs, traditions and land tenure systems of the indigenous peoples concerned (MV, p. 33).
19. BC, article 30 (II) (15).

Disclosure statement

No potential conflict of interest was reported by the author(s).

ORCID

María Itatí Dolhare http://orcid.org/0000-0003-3363-0394
Sol Rojas-Lizana http://orcid.org/0000-0002-9198-1005

References

Acosta, A. (2013). *El Buen Vivir: Sumak Kawsay, una oportunidad para imaginar otros mundos*. Icaria & Antrazyt.

Anaya, S. J. (2015). Report of the special rapporteur on the rights of indigenous peoples on extractive industries and indigenous peoples. *Arizona Journal International and Comparative Law, 32*(1), 110–141. https://scholar.law.colorado.edu/articles/33

Anghie, A., & Chimni, B. S. (2003). Third world approaches to international law and individual responsibility in internal conflict. *Chinese Journal of International Law, 2*(1), 77–103. https://doi.org/10.1093/oxfordjournals.cjilaw.a000480

Bolivia, Plurinational State of. (2009). *Constitution*. (Max Planck Institute, Trans.). (n.d.) La Paz: Project Constitute, Oxford University Press. https://www.constituteproject.org/constitution/Bolivia_2009?lang = en

Butleritchie, D. T. (2004). The confines of modern constitutionalism. *Pierce Law Review, 3*(1), 1–32. http://scholars.unh.edu/unh_lr/vol3/iss1/3

Caudillo Félix, G. A. (2012). El Buen Vivir: un diálogo intercultural. *Ra-Ximhai, 8*(2), 345–354. http://www.redalyc.org/articulo.oa?id=4612336601 https://doi.org/10.35197/rx.08.01.e.2012.14.gc

Chivi Vargas, I. (2010). Constitucionalismo emancipatorio, desarrollo normativo y jurisdicción indígena. In I. Chivi Vargas (Ed.), *Bolivia: nueva constitución política del estado – conceptos elementales para su desarrollo normativo* (pp. 73–90). Vicepresidencia del Estado Plurinacional de Bolivia.

Clavero, B. S. (2010). Bolivia entre el constitucionalismo colonial y constitucionalismo emancipatorio. In I. Chivi Vargas (Ed.), *Bolivia: nueva constitución política del estado – conceptos elementales para su desarrollo normativo* (pp. 97–108). Vicepresidencia del Estado Plurinacional de Bolivia.

Delgado Burgoa, R. E. (2010). Algunas reflexiones sobre la Constitución Política del Estado. In I. Chivi Vargas (Ed.), *Bolivia: nueva constitución política del estado – conceptos elementales para su desarrollo normativo* (pp. 39–55). Vicepresidencia del Estado Plurinacional de Bolivia.

De Sousa Santos, B. (2000). *Crítica de la razón indolente: para un nuevo sentido común: la ciencia, el derecho y la política en la transición paradigmática*. Editorial Desclee de Brouwer.

De Sousa Santos, B. (2002). *Toward a new legal common sense*. Butterworths Lexis Nexis.

De Sousa Santos, B. (2014). *Epistemologies of the south: Justice against epistemicide*. Paradigm Publishers.

Dolhare, M. I. (2019). *The concept of Vivir Bien (Living Well) and the constitutional recognition of indigenous epistemologies: towards a decolonising legal project* [PhD thesis]. The University of Queensland, Australia. https://doi.org/10.1017/jie.2017.31

Grosfoguel, R. (2013). The structure of knowledge in westernized universities: Epistemic racism/sexism and the four genocides/epistemicides of the long 16th century. *Human Architecture: Journal of the Sociology of Self-Knowledge, 11*(1), 73–90. http://scholarworks.umb.edu/humanarchitecture/vol11/iss1/8

Hall, M. A., & Wright, R. F. (2008). Systematic content analysis of judicial opinions. *California Law Review, 96*(1), 63–122. https://heinonline-org.ezproxy.library.uq.edu.au/HOL/P?h=hein.journals/calr96&i=71

Huanacuni Mamani, F. (2010). *Buen Vivir/Vivir Bien: Filosofía, políticas, estrategias y experiencias regionales andinas*. Convenio Andrés Bello. Instituto Internacional de Integración.

Lacroix, L. (2012). Indigenous territoriality and political agenda in Bolivia (1970-2010). *Revista de l'Institue Catala d' Antropologia, 17*(1), 60–77. https://halshs.archives-ouvertes.fr/halshs-00738479

Lee, D. (2001). *Cognitive linguistics: An introduction*. Oxford University Press.

Reisigl, M., & Wodak, R. (2001). *Discourse and discrimination: Rhetorics or racism and antisemitism*. Routledge.

Rojas-Lizana, S. (2019). *The discourse of perceived discrimination: Perspectives from contemporary Australian society*. Routledge.

Rojas-Lizana, S., & Dolhare, M. I. (2021). ¿Qué Importa el preámbulo?: pensamiento decolonial en el preámbulo de las constituciones de Bolivia y Ecuador: una aproximación desde el análisis del discurso. *Critical Discourse Studies, 18*(1), 43–75. https://doi.org/10.1080/17405904.2019.1567363

Teixeira Delgado, A. C. (2018). *Suma Qamaña* as a strategy of power: Politicizing the pluriverse. *Rev. Carta Inter. Belo Horizonte, 13*(3), 236–261. https://doi.org/10.21530/ci.v13n3.2018.818

Viciano Pastor, R., & Martínez Dalmau, R. (2010). Los procesos constituyentes latinoamericanos y el nuevo paradigma constitucional. *IUS. Revista del Instituto de Ciencias Jurídicas de Puebla, 25(4)*, 7–29. https://doi.org/10.35487/rius.v4i25.2010.214

Ward, T. (2011). The right to free, prior, and informed consent: Indigenous peoples' participation rights within international law. *Northwestern Journal of International Human Rights, 10*(2), 54–84. https://scholarlycommons.law.northwestern.edu/njihr/vol10/iss2/2

Westman, I. (2013). 'We value it because it is only on the earth that you can put your feet' – A case study of landscape values and perspectives in the Indigenous Territory and National Park Isiboro Secure highway conflict [Bachelor's thesis]. University of Gothenburg, Sweden.

OPEN ACCESS

Race, religion, law: An intertextual micro-genealogy of 'stirring up hatred' provisions in England and Wales

Jen Neller

ABSTRACT
This paper examines why there are different thresholds for the offences of stirring up racial hatred and stirring up religious hatred in the UK's Public Order Act 1986. Concepts of genealogy, intertextuality and problematisation are used to structure a critical discourse analysis that traces different understandings of race, religion, and racial and religious hatred across legal texts. The analysis reveals a rift between assertions within parliament that race is an immutable characteristic, and much more flexible and inclusive judicial understandings of race. This finding challenges justifications for the legislative discrepancy and points to more progressive possibilities.

Introduction

Literature on hate speech and the law is plentiful. The topic is often approached as a dilemma of competing values, with free speech and individual autonomy variously pitted against dignity, equality and other notions of group or individual harm (e.g. Baker, 1989; Brown, 2008; Coliver, 1992; Hare & Weinstein, 2009; Heinze, 2006; Matsuda et al., 1993; Thompson, 2012; Tsesis, 2009; Waldron, 2012). However, from critical and anticolonial perspectives, the pursuit of a single, universal answer to a normative question is problematic (Bhambra, 2014; Young, 1990). Such perspectives instead require attention to the particular: in this instance, the particular contexts in which certain speech is criminalised. With its emphasis on understanding texts in relation to their contexts of production (Van Dijk, 1994, p. 435), critical discourse analysis can be used to shift from the abstract, positivist debates that dominate the topic of hate speech law to more concrete, constructivist analyses.

The particular context with which this article is concerned is the 'stirring up hatred' provisions of the Public Order Act 1986 (POA). This legislation has been critiqued both for being too broad an incursion on free speech (Hare, 2006) and for being too narrow to be effective in the pursuit of equality (Goodall, 2007; Oyediran, 1992). But in addition to grounding debates on how values have and should be balanced, analysing legal texts allows other themes to emerge. Thus, this article focuses on questions of identity in the context of a distinction between racial and religious hatred within the POA. I begin by explaining how this distinction motivated a genealogical enquiry, which reaches back in time through interconnected texts. I then analyse three sets of legal texts:

- The primary text: relevant sections of the POA currently in force;
- Secondary texts: selected parliamentary debates on the enactment of the religious hatred provisions, which were added alongside the POA's racial hatred provisions in 2006.
- A tertiary text: the 1983 House of Lords judgment in the case of Mandla v Dowell Lee [1983] 2 WLR 620.

Through these texts, I follow a thread backwards in time to build a nuanced picture of how a particular legal issue – the distinction between racial and religious hatred – has been understood by lawmakers and judges in the UK.

Intertextual genealogy

Constructing a genealogy entails 'using history as a means of critical engagement with the present' (Garland, 2014, p. 367). Ordinarily, legal studies investigate the past to reveal the 'true' origins of something, and thereby to locate a historical authority to support a present assertion. In contrast, a genealogy investigates the past to reveal contradictions and contingencies, and thus to disrupt present beliefs (Foucault, 1984a, p. 82; see also Fairclough, 2013, p. 33). Thus, rather than starting with an artefact from the past and seeking to trace its influences over time, a genealogical study begins with a problem in the present and looks back through time to trace the conditions that brought it about (Garland, 2014, pp. 378–379; Foucault in Kritzman, 1988, p. 262). But this is not a purely destructive endeavour: by unsettling assumed trajectories, space is made to consider alternative possibilities for the future (Box & Simrell King, 2000).

After the initial diagnosis of a present concern, the notion of problematisation – how something comes to be regarded as a problem – continues to shape the enquiry (Foucault, 1984b, p. 389). Therefore, in this paper I investigate how the problematic stirring up hatred provisions were constructed and agreed upon as a solution, which in turn entails examining how racial and religious hatred have been problematised. More specifically, the focus is on discrepancies between the stirring up racial hatred offences, which are contained in Part III of the POA, and the stirring up religious hatred offences, which were added in 2006 as Part IIIA. The problem is ostensibly that the latter are more restrictive and thus more difficult to convict under. As considered below, it has been argued that this distinction is justified by a substantive difference between racial and religious hatred. However, the matter is complicated by the fact that stirring up hatred against Jews and Sikhs can currently be prosecuted under the wider racial hatred provisions, whereas stirring up hatred against other religious groups can only be prosecuted under the narrower religious hatred provisions. The discrepancy between Parts III and IIIA of the POA therefore establishes a distinction between racial and religious hatred that has been described as creating a 'hierarchy of hatred' (Law Commission, 2021, p. 394) and as failing to account for the ways in which race and religion may be experienced as indivisible (Meer, 2008; Idriss, 2002).

Through the methods of genealogy and problematisation, this paper seeks to understand the legal distinction between racial and religious hatred, not in relation to some ontological notion of what race, religion and racial/religious hatred *are*, but in relation to how they have been perceived and given meaning as legal categories. Law is therefore studied as both a social phenomenon and a discursive phenomenon. Although there may be many unwritten and unspoken modes by which law is produced and operates, and although meanings and significances shift and develop over time, legal texts provide a concrete dataset through which those shifts can be traced. It is these relationships that are encompassed by the term intertextuality, which refers how 'all texts are linked to other texts, both in the past and in the present' (Wodak, 2008, p. 3).

While all genealogies are intertextual insofar as they draw together a variety of texts, I use the term to describe a particular method for selecting a dataset. First, an intertextual genealogy requires a primary text which elucidates the problem to be investigated. Then, the texts that most directly influenced the primary text are selected as secondary texts. Then, the texts that most directly influenced the secondary texts in relation to the initial problem are selected as tertiary texts. And so on. This application of genealogy to intertextuality inverts the notion of 'textual travel' (Rock et al., 2013): rather than tracing the journeys and evolutions of a primary text through its iterations in *later* texts, a primary text is dissected so as to identify *earlier* texts that have 'travelled' into it.

Here, I have space to discuss only three sets of texts that I have selected for their intertextual connection to the initial problem: Parts III and IIIA of the POA (the primary text), relevant excerpts from the parliamentary debates on the Racial and Religious Hatred (RRH) Bill (secondary texts), and the House of Lords judgment in the *Mandla* case (a tertiary text). Far longer chains and far more complex webs could be constructed. However, I hope to demonstrate that even a micro-genealogy can prove insightful.

The primary text: the legislation

Part III of the Public Order Act 1986 (POA) is titled 'Racial Hatred'. Section 18(1) therein reads as follows:

> A person who uses threatening, abusive or insulting words or behaviour, or displays any written material which is threatening, abusive or insulting, is guilty of an offence if –
>
> (a) he intends thereby to stir up racial hatred, or
>
> (b) having regard to all the circumstances racial hatred is likely to be stirred up thereby

Sections 19–23 cover various other acts that are intended or likely to stir up racial hatred, including publishing, distributing, displaying, performing or broadcasting material that is threatening, abusive or insulting. From these provisions, the legislation appears to encompass racial hatred in all its forms, regardless of the identities of the victims or the perpetrators. However, s. 17 elaborates on the meaning of 'racial hatred':

> In this Part 'racial hatred' means hatred against a group of persons defined by reference to colour, race, nationality (including citizenship) or ethnic or national origins.

We might ask how this is to be determined. In a case brought under these provisions, must a group targeted by hate speech be found to 'objectively' fulfil this definition? If so, these provisions engage the law in scrutinising identity characteristics and classifying who *is* and who *is not* a member of a racial group. Such an understanding of race as fixed and objectively classifiable conflicts with more progressive views that race is socially determined and variable according to context (Hall, 1997; Meer, 2008; Powell, 1997). Alternatively, would it be sufficient for the hate speech itself to define its target group by reference to colour, race, nationality or ethnic or national origins? If so, scrutiny would fall on the hate speech rather than its targets; fulfilment of the s. 17 definition would depend on whether a targeted group had been *racialised* rather than whether they were deemed inherently 'racial'.

Let us now examine the religious hatred provisions. The Racial and Religious Hatred Act 2006 (RRH Act) added Part IIIA to the POA. Part IIIA has also, since 2008, been amended to include hatred on grounds of sexual orientation. Although there is much of interest in this addition, it is tangential to our focus on how racial and religious hatred have been distinguished. Part IIIA copies the structure of Part III but contains three significant discrepancies. Disregarding the 2008 additions pertaining to sexual orientation, s. 29B reads:

> A person who uses threatening words or behaviour, or displays any written material which is threatening, is guilty of an offence if he intends thereby to stir up religious hatred.

Compared with the corresponding text of s. 18(1) in Part III, s. 29B is narrower as it only encompasses threatening words or behaviour, and not also that which is abusive or insulting. Secondly, it is necessary to demonstrate that there was intent to stir up religious hatred; this is not always required in relation to racial hatred as it can alternatively be demonstrated that hatred was likely to be stirred up.[1] The third discrepancy arises from s. 29J in Part IIIA:

> Nothing in this Part shall be read or given effect in a way which prohibits or restricts discussion, criticism or expressions of antipathy, dislike, ridicule, insult or abuse of particular religions or the beliefs or practices of their adherents, or of any other belief system or the beliefs or practices of its adherents, or proselytising or urging adherents of a different religion or belief system to cease practising their religion or belief system.

There is no corresponding 'free speech' provision in relation to racial hatred.

A final point to note is that Part IIIA also contains a section on the meaning of 'religious hatred': s 29A states that,

> In this Part 'religious hatred' means hatred against a group of persons defined by reference to religious belief or lack of religious belief.

Here, we can raise the same query as to whether a group of persons must be identified as religious by some purportedly objective determination or by the hate speech itself. If the hatred is explicitly against Christians, Muslims or Hindus, for example, this ambiguity is likely to be inconsequential. If, however, the hatred is against women who wear headscarves, for example, then it is indeed consequential. Headscarves are widely enough associated with Islam in the UK that hatred against their wearers could be religious hatred. However, women from many different religions wear headscarves, while others choose such attire due to culture, hair loss or fashion. Therefore, 'women who wear headscarves' cannot be classified as 'a group of persons defined by reference to religious belief'. This example illustrates the significance of context in understanding hate speech and the difficulty of pre-determining who can and cannot be victims of a particular type of hatred.

While the separation of the religious hatred provisions from the racial hatred provisions in the POA is apparent, close analysis enables the precise contours of this distinction to be mapped, raising questions of not only why the distinction has been drawn in these particular ways, but also of the extent to which it reflects a tendency to view identity characteristics as fixed and objectively discernible. These questions inform the following inquiry into the secondary texts.

The secondary texts: parliamentary debates

Legislative texts are shaped by the parliamentary debates in which they were scrutinised, amended and ultimately approved; these debates therefore comprise a useful source of insight into the particularities of specific legislation. Moreover, as parliamentarians aim both to influence the opinions of their peers and to be seen as representative of wider public opinion, parliamentary debates provide an index of perspectives and norms at a particular time and in relation to a particular topic (Johnson & Vanderbeck, 2014, p. 4; Lunny, 2017, p. 3; Thompson, 2016, p. 92).

In his introduction to the second reading of the Racial and Religious Hatred (RRH) Bill in the House of Commons, the then Home Secretary, Charles Clarke, stated that the stirring up religious hatred provisions 'had been agreed by the House twice previously: as part of the Anti-Terrorism, Crime and Security Act 2001 and, only a few months ago, as part of the Serious Organised Crime and Police Act 2005' (HC Deb 21 June 2005, co. 668). While there were concerns in 2001 that it was unwise to include religious hatred provisions within emergency anti-terrorism legislation, the provisions were more deeply debated during the passage of the Serious Organised Crime and Police (SOCP) Bill. The SOCP Bill proposed amending Part III of the POA to place stirring up religious hatred on an equal footing with stirring up racial hatred. This was rejected by the House of Lords, which led to the removal of the provisions from the Bill to secure its passage before the 2005 general election. Labour included the religious hatred provisions within their election manifesto, and once re-elected the Labour Government reproduced the SOCP Bill's amendments to Part III in a new RRH Bill. However, the Lords rejected this again and counter proposed Part IIIA. The Government accepted the separation of the offences and the addition of the free speech provision but asked the Commons to reject the more restrictive speech and intent thresholds. In two extremely close divisions, the Government was outvoted and the Lords' amendments were all accepted.

These events suggest that the legislative differentiation between racial and religious hatred originated in the House of Lords. However, how it was rationalised remains unclear. Analysis of the secondary texts reveals that the debates on the religious hatred offences were deeply convoluted and complicated by misunderstandings as well as disagreements. In this situation, problematisation provides a means of unravelling the tangled threads. Three main framings of the problem – to which the RRH Bill was presented as a solution – structure the remainder of this section. I call these the formal, substantive and rhetorical problems.

The formal problem: inequality before the law

The problem of inequality before the law was described in Clarke's assertion that,

> The Bill seeks to address the anomaly that means that Jews and Sikhs are protected under the existing law, but that other faith groups, and people of no faith, are not protected. (HC Deb 21 June 2005, col. 678)

This framing of the problem was widely affirmed in parliament. The apparent anomaly was said to be the result of the racial hatred provisions being extended by case law. However, the case law referred to was the 1983 judgment in *Mandla v Dowell Lee*, which predated the enactment of the POA in 1986. Therefore, the 'anomaly' had been endorsed by parliament when it passed Part III. Nevertheless, the logic was that when the court established in *Mandla* that Sikhs – like Jews – comprise a group defined by reference to ethnic origins, Sikhs became encompassed within the stirring up racial hatred provisions by virtue of s. 17 of the POA (and its earlier equivalent). This was expressed in the debates as the inclusion within racial hatred provisions of mono-ethnic religious groups, as compared to multi-ethnic religious groups. Such perspectives, which were backed by the Government, belie a belief that a legal determination of whether a group is categorically 'defined by reference to race' (including ethnic origins) establishes whether hatred against that group is 'racial hatred'. Indeed, the immutability of race was asserted repeatedly throughout the debates. As then Conservative MP Boris Johnson put it, 'It is obvious that there is a category difference between one's race, which is a question of nature, and one's religion, which is a matter of choice' (HC Deb 21 June 2005, col. 732). Immutability does seem to be implied by the term 'ethnic *origins*' in s. 17; yet since s. 17 also includes citizenship, it cannot be held that racial hatred can only be hatred of unchangeable characteristics.

For others, the mono/multi-ethnic framing was unsatisfactory. During earlier attempts to enact religious hatred provisions, Lord Lester argued that there was not in fact any anomaly or inequality between the treatment of different religious groups (henceforth referred to as 'the Lester argument'). With support in the House of Commons from Conservative MP Dominic Grieve and Liberal Democrat MP Evan Harris, Lester's position was that existing law provided no protection against incitement to religious hatred of any group, but provided protection against incitement to racial hatred for all groups. This responded to the Government's concern that far-right organisations were referring to religious groups in order to evade the racial hatred offences. The Lester argument asserted that such hatred should be classified as racial since it was 'not making a theological point, but a racist one' (Harris, HC Deb 21 June 2005, col. 740). Therefore, the only solution required was clarification, via an amendment to s. 17, that the stirring up of racial hatred through reference to religion would be caught by Part III. Conversely, expressions of hatred that addressed religious beliefs were argued to be beyond the proper remit of criminal law.

The Lester argument was exceptional for advocating scrutiny of the hatred rather than its targets, and Grieve also acknowledged that religion may contribute to racial identity

(HC Deb 28 June, col. 11). However, the argument is premised on a distinction – and hierarchy – between racial and religious hatred that limits the latter to statements about the doctrine or practice of a religion. Hatred stirred up against a religious group which cannot conceivably be classified as racial hatred, such as sectarian hatred or hatred against converts, is not accounted for. Thus, the Lester argument sought to redraw the line between racial and religious hatred but was limited in its engagement with the substantive problem of religious hatred, to which we turn next.

The substantive problem: religious hatred

Other framings of the problem focused less on the technicality of the law and more on lived experiences that showed religious hatred to be a significant and harmful phenomenon. Such arguments often directly challenged the aforementioned distinction between race as immutable and religion as chosen. Several speakers noted that an individual cannot change the fact that they were born into a certain religion, the religiosity of their upbringing or the religious identity of their family. For example, Labour MP Shahid Malik emphasised how an individual has little control over the racial or religious group to which they are *perceived* as belonging:

> When I was beaten to a pulp by a gang of skinheads on my first day at high school, it was not because of my religion. They did not know or care whether I was a Christian, Hindu or Muslim ... In those days we were all seen as "Pakis" and we were all fair game. ... Now, when I receive anonymous hate mail or the family car is firebombed in the middle of the night, or when abuse is hurled from cars that whisk by, or I am surrounded by a gang of 20 thugs from Combat 18 telling me that I am going to die, it is because I am a Muslim. Whether I choose it or not, I am defined by others in terms of my religion, and by my perceived culture. (HC Deb 21 June 2005, col. 703)

Furthermore, Baroness Ramsay (HL 11 October 2005, col. 208) referred to sectarianism in Northern Ireland to emphasise the harms of religious hatred quite apart from any entanglements with race. It was also argued that the ability to change religion was irrelevant. For example, Baroness Whitaker (HL Deb 11 October 2005, cols. 214–215) questioned 'why should we want a society where people have to do that to be accepted without hatred?' Thus, some advocates of the Bill argued that experiences of religious hatred are equivalent to experiences of racial hatred and therefore warrant equal redress.

However, a more subtle distinction between race and religion can be positioned in response to the purported irrelevance of mutability. This is the argument that criticism of race is nonsensical and undesirable in all situations, whereas criticism of religion can be rational. For example, Labour MP Robert Marshall-Andrews stated:

> Nobody can say to me that I ought to be black, white, Chinese or Russian, but there is no shortage of people outside this House, and some inside it, who would have no hesitation in saying that I ought to be Christian, Islamic, or Jewish. (HC Deb 31 Jan 2006, cols. 231–232)

While often conflating criticism and hatred, this argument highlights a more convincing substantive difference between race and religion, which could point to different understandings of *what amounts to hatred* in relation to these characteristics. To say that I am offended by your religious beliefs is clearly not the same as to say that I am offended by the colour of your skin. Such a distinction could justify some legal discrepancy, such as the additional free speech provision of s. 29JA. However, this argument does not respond to the anecdotal evidence that *stirring up hatred* against groups defined by reference to race or religion produces commensurate harms. Moreover, hatred may not fall clearly into one or the other category as 'there are many people for whom an easy distinction between religion and race is not accurate' (Clarke, HC Deb 21 June 2005, col 676) and 'race, religion and culture are in truth intimately intertwined' (Denham, HC Deb 21 June 2005, col. 678).

The rhetorical problem: minority frustrations

Rather than viewing religious hatred as a problem in and of itself, a third framing presented it as detrimental to 'race relations', 'integration' and 'public order'. Here, the religious hatred provisions were presented as important for making certain groups – predominantly identified as Muslim – feel that their concerns were being taken seriously (Brown, 2017). For example, Lord Hannay presented the RRH Bill as a transaction in efforts to combat Islamist extremism:

> If we cannot legislate in a scrupulously even-handed way towards our Muslim compatriots, making it clear that they and we face the same laws and receive the same protection under those laws, how on earth are we to persuade them to work with us against this perverted and paranoiac ideology which has taken root in their midst? (HL Deb 11 October 2005, col 256)

There was thus an elision in some quarters of parliament between problematising religious hatred and problematising those who it targets. This was especially prominent among opponents of the RRH Bill who described it as a 'sop to the Muslim community' (Baron, HC Deb 21 June 2005, col, 745; see also Johnson, HC Deb 21 June 2005, col. 732; O'Cathain, HL Deb 11 October 2005, col. 210; Flather, HL Deb 11 October 2005, col. 216). There is a lot more to be unpacked here about racialisation, minoritisation and the problematisation of difference. However, this perspective provides little insight into the distinction between racial and religious hatred, aside from perhaps that it was more important to be seen to do something than nothing, even if it was ultimately more symbolism than substance (Goodall, 2007).

The tertiary text: the Mandla case

Analysis of the secondary texts reveals complex and conflicting views about the nature of racial and religious hatred, but a pervading belief in the immutability of race shines through. In light of this, the House of Lords *Mandla* judgment is taken as a tertiary text within this micro-genealogy for two reasons: first, to consider the extent to which this judgment informed the dominant perception in parliament that a court can determine whether a group is inherently 'racial'; and second, to evaluate contrasting interpretations of the judgment whereby it was understood either to have contributed to a legal discrepancy in the treatment of religious groups or it was denied that such a discrepancy existed, as per the Lester argument.

The legal provisions at issue in *Mandla* were not the stirring up racial hatred provisions but the anti-discrimination provisions of the Race Relations Act 1976 (RRA). The statutory language at issue, however, is identical: s. 3(1) of the RRA defines a racial group as 'a group of persons defined by reference to colour, race, nationality or ethnic or national origins'. The case concerned whether a school's prohibition on wearing turbans could constitute racial discrimination against Sikhs, leading the Lords to focus on the question of whether Sikhs *are* a group defined by reference to their ethnic origins. To this extent, the Lords sought to determine the 'correct' classification of the group. In other ways, however, the leading judgments of Lords Fraser and Templeton significantly diverged from the notion that membership of a racial group is necessarily an immutable fact and emphasised the role of perception in racial identity. It is worth quoting a passage of Lord Fraser's judgment at length:

> For a group to constitute an ethnic group in the sense of the Act of 1976, it must, in my opinion, regard itself, and be regarded by others, as a distinct community by virtue of certain characteristics. ... The conditions which appear to me to be essential are these: (1) a long shared history, of which the group is conscious as distinguishing it from other groups, and the memory of which it keeps alive; (2) a cultural tradition of its own, including family and social customs and manners, often but not necessarily associated with religious observance. In addition to those two essential characteristics the following characteristics are, in my opinion, relevant; (3) either a common geographical origin, or descent from a small number of common ancestors; (4) a common language, not necessarily peculiar to the group; (5) a common literature peculiar to the group; (6) a common religion different from that of neighbouring groups or from the general community surrounding it; (7) being a minority or being an oppressed or a dominant group within a larger community. (p. 562)

This broad and flexible framework is oriented around being subjectively regarded as a distinct community and, in finding that a shared religion can contribute to ethnicity, blurs the line between racial and religious identity. Moreover, Fraser explicitly challenged the notion of race as a biological fact:

> My Lords, I recognise that "ethnic" conveys a flavour of race but it cannot, in my opinion, have been used in the Act of 1976 in a strictly racial or biological sense. For one thing, it would be absurd to suppose that Parliament can have intended that membership of a particular racial group should depend upon scientific proof that a person possessed the relevant distinctive biological characteristics (assuming that such characteristics exist). ... the briefest glance at the evidence in this case is enough to show that, within the human race, there are very few, if any, distinctions which are scientifically recognised as racial. (p. 561)

This aspect of the judgment, it seems, did not 'travel' into the parliamentary debates on the RRH Bill.

The judgment affirmed that Jews and Sikhs are groups defined by reference to ethnic origins, but neither endorsed nor foreclosed the possibility that other religious groups might also be. While it was recognised by some parliamentarians that hatred directed against Muslims could be racial in nature, the notion that Muslims might be regarded as a group defined by ethnic origins was not entertained. Yet, there were 50 references to the 'Muslim community' within the secondary texts, suggesting that Muslims might, even within those debates, have been 'regarded by others as a distinct community' (Dobe & Chhokar, 2000; Idriss, 2002).

Conclusions

This paper has sought to better understand the discrepancies between the racial and religious hatred provisions of the POA. Through a genealogical approach, the aim has not been to seek *the* definitive answer to a question, but to explore a plurality of understandings. To this end, the intertextual method of data selection has proved a useful means of circumscribing the study (which could be extended in many directions) and the concept of problematisation has proved useful for delineating specific arguments.

On the initial question of the current discrepancy between the racial and religious hatred provisions, the genealogy has not found a coherent and persuasive rationale. It is shown instead that the RRH Act failed on its own terms: the Government set out to equalise the redress available to different religious groups but ultimately upheld the legal distinction between them. While *criticism* of a person's race and religion may be qualitatively different, no evidence was produced in parliament or in the *Mandla* case to suggest that the stirring up of racial or religious *hatred* against a group produces qualitatively different harms.

A second question emerged from close analysis of the primary text, which found that it would be possible to interpret the provisions defining racial and religious hatred either as requiring a targeted group to be classified as inherently 'defined by reference to' race or religion, or as requiring the hate speech itself to define its targets as such. Analysis of the secondary texts indicates that the positivist interpretation dominated in parliament during the passage of the stirring up religious hatred provisions (with the exception of the Lester argument) and the notion that race is an immutable 'fact' prevailed. However, the tertiary text provides judicial authority in support of far more nuanced interpretations. Thus, a seismic rift has been identified between the understandings of race presented by the House of Lords while exercising its judicial functions in 1983 and while exercising its parliamentary functions in 2005/6, with the earlier perspective being the more progressive of the two.

The intention here is not to highlight misrepresentations of the *Mandla* judgment in parliament as an error in an otherwise rational system. Rather, the analysis demonstrates the folly of seeking consistent logics, a coherent trajectory or a singular 'truth'. It shows how law that is intended to advance equality can end up entrenching inequality and how law that is supposed to combat racism can essentialise and entrench divisions. More specifically, this study has shown the propensity for understandings of race as an immutable classification to prevail within parliament, but also that there is scope – both within the legislative text and through judicial authority – to contest this framing and adopt more flexible and inclusive approaches. This paper therefore illustrates how attention to intertextuality can destabilise assumptions and uncover alternatives. Indeed, the ongoing need for such alternatives has been demonstrated by the Law Commission's recent consultation report on UK hate crime law, which continues to ascribe a distinction between 'ethnoreligious' groups and 'multi-ethnic' religious groups to *Mandla* and proclaims that 'Race is unquestionably and wholly immutable' (2021, p. 393). For many reasons, law is a blunt and limited tool in the pursuit of a more egalitarian society, but this paper shows one small area where a step back from the reproduction and entrenchment of outdated views on racial difference is possible.

Note

1. However, this discrepancy is complicated by s. 18(5) of Part III.

Disclosure statement

No potential conflict of interest was reported by the author(s).

References

Baker, C. E. (1989). *Human liberty and freedom of speech*. Oxford University Press.
Bhambra, G. (2014). Postcolonial and decolonial dialogues. *Postcolonial Studies*, *17*(2), 115–121. https://doi.org/10.1080/13688790.2014.966414
Box, R., & Simrell King, C. (2000). The 'T'ruth is elsewhere: Critical history. *Administrative Theory and Praxis*, *22*(4), 751–771. https://doi.org/10.1080/10841806.2000.11643489
Brown, A. (2008). The racial and religious hatred act 2006: A millian response. *Critical Review of International Social and Political Philosophy*, *11*(1), 1–24. https://doi.org/10.1080/13698230701880471
Brown, A. (2017). The politics behind the introduction of stirring up religious hatred offences in England and Wales. *Politics, Religion and Ideology*, *18*(1), 42–72. https://doi.org/10.1080/21567689.2017.1303770
Coliver, S. (1992). *Striking a balance: Hate speech, freedom of expression and non-discrimination*. Article 19 & Human Rights Centre, University of Essex.
Dobe, K., & Chhokar, S. (2000). Muslims, ethnicity and the law. *International Journal of Discrimination and the Law*, *4*(4), 369–386. https://doi.org/10.1177/135822910000400404
Fairclough, N. (2013). *Critical discourse analysis: The critical study of language* (2nd ed.). Routledge.
Foucault, M. (1984a). Nietzsche, genealogy, history. In P. Rabinow (Ed.), *The Foucault reader* (pp. 76–101). Pantheon Books.
Foucault, M. (1984b). Polemics, politics and problematizations: An interview with Michel Foucault. By P. Rabinow. In P. Rabinow (Ed.), *The Foucault reader* (pp. 381–390). Pantheon Books.
Garland, D. (2014). What is a 'history of the present'? On Foucault's genealogies and their critical pre-conditions. *Punishment and Society*, *16*(4), 365–384. https://doi.org/10.1177/1462474514541711
Goodall, K. (2007). Incitement to religious hatred: All talk and no substance? *Modern Law Review*, *70*(1), 89–113. https://doi.org/10.1111/j.1468-2230.2006.00627.x
Hall, S. (1997). Race, the floating signifier: What more is there to say about race? In P. Gilroy & R. Wilson Gilmore (Eds.), *Selected writings on race and difference* (pp. 359–373). Duke University Press.
Hare, I. (2006). Crosses, crescents and sacred cows: Criminalising incitement to religious hatred. *Public Law*, (Autumn), 521–538.
Hare, I., & Weinstein, J. (Eds.). (2009). *Extreme speech and democracy*. Oxford University Press.
Heinze, E. (2006). Viewpoint absolutism and hate speech. *Modern Law Review*, *69*(4), 543–582. https://doi.org/10.1111/j.1468-2230.2006.00599.x
Idriss, M. (2002). Religion and the anti-terrorism, crime and security act 2001. *Criminal Law Review*, (November), 890–911.
Johnson, P., & Vanderbeck, R. (2014). *Law, religion and homosexuality*. Routledge.
Kritzman, L. (1988). Power and sex: An interview with Michel Foucault. In L. Kritzman (Ed.), *Michel Foucault: Politics, philosophy, culture: Interviews and other writings, 1977–1984* (pp. 110–124). Routledge.
Law Commission. (2021). *Hate crime laws: Final report*. Law Com No 402. https://www.lawcom.gov.uk/project/hate-crime/
Lunny, A. (2017). *Hate crime: Language, legislatures and the law in Canada*. UBC Press.
Matsuda, M., Lawrence, C., Delgado, R., & Williams Crenshaw, K. (Eds.). (1993). *Words that wound: Critical race theory, assaultive speech and the first amendment*. Westview Press.

Meer, Nasar. (2008). The politics of voluntary and involuntary identities: are Muslims in Britain an ethnic, racial or religious minority?. *Patterns of Prejudice*, *42*(1), 61–81. https://doi.org/10.1080/00313220701805901

Oyediran, J. (1992). The United Kingdom's compliance with article 4 of the international convention on the elimination of all forms of racial discrimination. In S. Coliver (Ed.), *Striking a balance: Hate speech, freedom of expression and non-discrimination* (pp. 245–257). Article 19 & Human Rights Centre, University of Essex.

Powell, J. (1997). The 'racing' of American society: Race functioning as a verb before signifying as a noun. *Law and Inequality*, *15*(1), 99–125.

Rock, F, Heffer, C, & John, C. (2013). Introduction. In C. Heffer, F. Rock and J. Conley (Ed.), Legal-lay communication: Textual travels in the law. New York: Oxford University Press.

Thompson, N. (2016). To see ourselves: The rhetorical construction of an ideal citizenry in the perorations of twentieth-century budget speeches. *British Politics*, *12*(1), 90–114. https://doi.org/10.1057/s41293-016-0025-5

Thompson, S. (2012). Freedom of expression and hatred of religion. *Ethnicities*, *12*(2), 215–232. https://doi.org/10.1177/1468796811431298

Tsesis, A. (2009). Dignity and speech: The regulation of hate speech in a democracy. *Wake Forest Law Review*, *44*, 497–532.

Van Dijk, T. (1994). Critical discourse analysis. *Discourse & Society*, *5*(4), 435–436. https://doi.org/10.1177/0957926594005004001

Waldron, J. (2012). *The harm in hate speech*. Harvard University Press.

Wodak, R. (2008). Introduction: Discourse studies – important concepts and terms. In R. Wodak & M. Krzyzanowski (Eds.), *Qualitative discourse analysis in the social sciences* (pp. 1–24). Palgrave Macmillan.

Young, I. (1990). *Justice and the politics of difference*. Princeton University Press.

The Magna Carta of women as the Philippine translation of the CEDAW: A feminist critical discourse analysis

Gay Marie Manalo Francisco

ABSTRACT
Republic Act 9710, or the Magna Carta of Women (MCW), is considered the Philippine version or national law translation of the Convention on the Elimination of All Forms of Discrimination against Women (CEDAW). Using the concept of impact translation as a framework and the Feminist Critical Discourse Analysis (FCDA) approach, this article examines the MCW and the minutes of committee meetings, particularly the bicameral conference committee meeting where lawmakers agreed on the finalized version of the bill. It applies the concept of gender relationality in examining how legislators negotiated the provisions of the MCW, particularly those on reproductive health and the definition of gender. The analysis shows that these provisions challenged Catholic doctrines specifically on gender, childbearing, and pre-marital sexual relations. It argues that the Catholic conception of gender norms and women's role in society shaped the law's final version, disregarding the CEDAW Committee recommendations on abortion. Findings suggest that the legislators' fear that the law's ratification would serve as an opening for the legalization of abortion led to a weakened version of the law, particularly the section on women's reproductive health.

Introduction

This article focuses on the Magna Carta of Women (MCW), which is regarded as the Philippine version of the Convention on the Elimination of All Forms of Discrimination Against Women (CEDAW). The United Nations General Assembly adopted the CEDAW in 1979, and it became an international treaty in 1981. In keeping with the principles of CEDAW, the MCW is envisioned to be a comprehensive women's human rights law, which aims to eliminate discrimination through the recognition, protection, fulfillment, and promotion of Filipino women's rights. Zwingel (2013) refers to the CEDAW as 'the cornerstone of the international women's rights discourse for over 30 years' (p.111). Englehart and Miller (2014) aver that while CEDAW has weaker enforcement mechanisms than other human rights treaties, its goals are more encompassing. It covers public and private domains, urging states parties to carry out extensive gender equity policy changes.

This article examines how the Philippines translated the CEDAW to its national law, the MCW. Using Feminist Critical Discourse Analysis (FCDA), it studies the deliberations during the bicameral conference committee meeting where lawmakers agreed on the finalized version of the bill to be presented to the Senate and House of Representatives for transmission to the President. Specifically, it applies the concept of gender relationality (Lazar, 2000, 2007) in examining how legislators negotiated the disagreeing[1] provisions of the MCW bill. It asks the following questions: Which CEDAW articles and Committee recommendations were not adopted in the MCW? How was the non-adoption of recommendations rationalized or justified by the legislators? How did lawmakers conceptualize the disagreeing provisions of the bill, and how did these conceptualizations shape the law?

The first part of the article explains Zwingel's (2016) concept of impact translation. It then provides a brief history of the CEDAW and the MCW. The third section presents the FCDA and its benefit to analyze a women's rights law translated from an international convention and describes the methodology. Finally, it discusses the findings, focusing on the disagreeing provisions of the bill.

Impact translation: CEDAW and the Philippine women's rights law

Diffusion theorizes that international norms spread to local contexts engendering similarity among institutions. On the other hand, translation looks at how the local context makes sense of and activates international norms (Draude, 2017). In her work focusing on the diffusion of international women's rights, Savery (2007) argues that the states' 'gender-biased corporate identity' serves as the main hurdle in diffusion. In a comparative study of Germany, Spain, Japan, and India—countries which are very different in terms of society and culture—findings reveal that historical and contextual factors shape diffusion. While Savery (2007) highlights significant points in understanding diffusion and the barriers to states parties' adoption of international gender norms, there is little discussion of how governments translated these norms in their contexts. For instance, in discussing Japan's marginal policy improvements in response to CEDAW, it is unclear how specific policies were prioritized over others and what factors shaped these policies. Hence, there is a need to examine policy changes from the perspective of translation and not merely diffusion. More recent scholarship on norm diffusion is shifting towards 'multi-directionality' (Zwingel, 2016), leading to the concept of translation.

Norm diffusion seems to imply a unidirectional process (Zwingel, 2016). Draude (2017) acknowledges the 'linear paths of diffusion research' and argues against norm diffusion being a 'top-down process' (p. 588). Acharya's (2004) work on norm diffusion on security and humanitarian intervention in the Association of Southeast Asian Nations (ASEAN) concludes that local agents adjust transnational norms to suit prevailing practices and local conditions. Hence, Zwingel (2016) argues that translation is the more appropriate term to use 'to grasp multi-directionality' (p. 31).

Zwingel (2016) differentiates between 'global discourse translation' and 'impact translation.' The former focuses on the international level, specifically, how actors utilize institutions for collaborative action to form global norms. She cites CEDAW as an example of global discourse translation. Being more context-specific, 'impact translation' considers domestic actors, their perspectives, and actions, whether in support of or contrary to global norms.

Only a handful of countries are not parties to the CEDAW. Vatican City, Iran, Somalia, and Tonga did not sign the CEDAW, while the United States and Palau signed but have not ratified the treaty. Given the number of states parties, it would seem that the CEDAW has the potential to resolve most questions concerning women's rights, particularly on the issue of discrimination. Yet, the number of reservations by states parties proves that conceptions of what constitutes women's rights may vary between and among states—even when they have agreed in principle to an international treaty. Studies show that governments and their instrumentalities define key principles of the CEDAW differently despite being states parties. Some ideas conflict with traditions and religious views (Brandt & Kaplan, 1995; Savery, 2007; Weiss, 2003; Zwingel, 2012). Baldez (2011) maintains that the CEDAW is a valuable measure of women's interest despite its shortcomings since it enjoys support from most states. Unlike other measures of gender equality, CEDAW has a regular monitoring process, which gives importance to the context in its interchange with states parties (Liebowitz & Zwingel, 2014).

FCDA: examining discourse on women's rights in the law

Using FCDA allows for a comprehensive examination of the MCW, a law envisioned to eliminate all forms of discrimination against Filipino women. In the process of 'translation,' it is necessary to determine how legislators' discourses shaped the final law. As argued by Lazar (2005b), the focus of FCDA is 'on how gender ideology and gendered relations of power are (re)produced, negotiated and contested in representations of social practices, in social relationships between people, and in people's social and personal identities in texts and talk' (p. 11). Studies on women's rights legislation find that institutions such as the legislature and its internal structures, such as the various committees have gendered rules and practices. Using a gender lens in examining institutions reveals how gender shapes everyday processes of conceptualization and interaction in ways that breed inequalities against women (Acker, 1992). As scholars point out, while many rules are gendered, such as they affect men and women differently, most of these rules are gender blind, and they tend to obscure the established inequalities that have become embedded in the system (Childs, 2013; Curtin, 2018; Kenny, 2007; Mackay et al., 2010; Mackay & Waylen, 2009; Minto & Mergaert, 2018; Thomson, 2018).

Lazar (2005a, 2007, 2014) offers five fundamental principles for a feminist discourse praxis: feminist analytical activism, gender as ideological structure, the complexity of gender and power relations, discourse in the (de)construction of gender, and critical reflexivity as praxis. For this article, I focus on Lazar's concept of gender relationality and apply this principle to discuss the lawmakers' arguments in rationalizing their position for or against the CEDAW articles and Committee recommendations. Gender relationality examines the dynamics of gender discourse of women and men in identified groups (Lazar, 2000, 2007). It does not place women and men in separate camps but looks at how they 'co-construct' gender. It also includes studying how women interact with other women in these groups. Lazar (2007) refers to this as 'dynamics of forms of masculinity.' Women may work together to strengthen the support for equality or help encourage practices that discriminate against other women. I explored how the members of the bicameral conference committee, composed of women and men, negotiated the contentious provisions of the women's rights law. Using the framework, I analyzed the arguments, particularly noting discourses that support or contradict each other.

For the methodology, I referred to the CEDAW articles and the August 2006 CEDAW Committee concluding comments. The 2006 concluding comments presented the Committee recommendations for the Philippines as a state party. I then examined the text of the Republic Act No. 9710 'An Act Providing for the Magna Carta of Women' to determine which Committee recommendations were excluded from the law. After identifying the excluded provisions, I studied the minutes of the committee meetings, focusing on the bicameral conference committee meeting of the Senate and House of Representatives, taking note of the recommendations that legislators decided to exclude from the MCW and the arguments justifying the exclusion. I noted the ideas and concepts that lawmakers used to explain their stand on the contested provisions.

I primarily examined the bicameral conference committee[2] meeting on the disagreeing provisions of the MCW bill for three reasons (1) It was the venue for the House of Representatives and the Senate to prepare a conference report which paved the way for a finalized version of the bill for transmission to the President. In theory, conferees are prevented from removing provisions agreed to by both Houses to the effect of including new provisions (2) The contentious provisions include those that faced significant scrutiny in both chambers. Official records show that lawmakers decided to defer the discussion of these provisions during committee meetings and let the bicameral conference committee decide on them (3) It was the final opportunity to argue for the inclusion or removal of the contested provisions.

There were six disagreeing provisions between the House and Senate versions of the bill[3] (*Bicameral Conference Committee on the Disagreeing Provisions of House Bill 4273 and Senate Bill 2396 Re Magna Carta of Women*, 2009). However, the provisions on the definition of gender, equal access and elimination of discrimination in education, scholarships, and training, and women's right to health required the most extended deliberation. This article focuses on these three provisions.

Results and discussion

The Philippine CEDAW translation addressed all the major points in the CEDAW Committee recommendation in the MCW except those on divorce and abortion stated explicitly in paragraphs 28 and 32 of the August 2006 Concluding comments of the Committee on the Elimination of Discrimination against Women. The bill under review excluded matters deemed prohibited by existing Philippine statutes. While lawmakers generally had no issues incorporating other CEDAW recommendations, those related to abortion were generally avoided. The deliberations presupposed that lawmakers were barred from discussing these recommendations, deemed unconstitutional. Presupposition is a 'skilful way by which authors are able to imply meanings without overtly stating them, or present things as taken for granted and stable when in fact they may be contestable and ideological' (Machin & Mayr, 2012, p. 137). Abortion is considered a criminal act under Philippine law to date.[4] While the MCW does not specifically mention the word divorce, under Section 19, it provides for the Equal Rights in All Matters Relating to Marriage and Family Relations. This section includes 'the same rights to enter into and leave marriages or common law relationships referred to under the Family Code'.[5]

Resolving the Law's Contentious Provisions

On Reproductive Health

Based on my analysis, reproductive health is an area that has faced considerable opposition. The aversion of lawmakers, most of them men, to the word 'abortion' is evident. Table 1 illustrates the fear of lawmakers, especially the male lawmakers, to incorporate any concept that may be construed as consenting to or tolerating abortion or abortifacient means of family planning. In the following excerpts, Congresswoman Janet Garin, a medical doctor, explained the necessity of including abortion complications in the section on state provisions for women's reproductive health. Despite her medical expertise, her suggestion was overruled, and the male legislators prevailed. Instead, the Committee agreed to use the term 'pregnancy-related complications' in the final version of the bill.

The opposition on provisions, particularly those on women's reproductive health, were mainly from organizations associated with the Catholic Church. These groups fear that the law would be used to support the legalization of abortion. This excerpt, from the speech of Lucy Luistro, a representative of the Alliance for the Family Foundation of the Philippines, is one such example:

> Reproductive rights mean that contraception and abortion are framed as rights of women resulting from the woman's exclusive decision to choose whether to have children or not. While we are also committed to safeguard the dignity of women, we oppose any suggestion that childbearing is a form of discrimination or oppression that is grouped together with such

Table 1. Analysis of the Discussion on the Management of Complications Arising from Unsafe Abortions using Gender Relationality (Lazar, 2000, 2007).

Gender Relationality's Focus on Two Types of Relationships (Lazar, 2000, 2007)	The Bicameral Conference Committee Meeting on the Contentious Provisions of the Magna Carta of Women
Discursive *co-constructions* of ways of doing and being a woman and a man in particular communities of practice	**Reproductive Health: On the Management of Complications Arising from Unsafe Abortions**
Those who argued against using the term abortion complications were all men (three lawmakers). Despite the medical expertise of Dr. Garin, a woman legislator, her recommendation was overruled.	*Congressman Zialcita:* Most of the people who will read the Magna Carta are not doctors, they are not lawyers, they are ordinary people so when they use the word, prevention of abortion and abortion complications, they might get the impression that we are promoting abortion.
The woman lawmaker agreed with the Catholic conceptualization of abortion 'it's a sin' but appealed to the moral duty to 'save a life.'	*Congresswoman Janet Garin:* Because this provision is supposed to address management of abortion complications and, again, I defer to the rationale that a person who underwent even induced abortion, it's a sin. But once they are on the brink of death after a complication, still, it is the duty of anybody to manage that complication because that's part of saving a life.
Co-constructing abortion as a prohibited act but using 'Christian' traits to rationalize the government's support for women who suffer abortion complications	A male lawmaker agreed with Congresswoman Garin but recommended the use of the term pregnancy-related complications, documenting that pregnancy-related complications would include post-abortion complications. The lawmaker used the analogy of the 'Christian act of bringing a wounded rebel to a medical facility.'
Dynamics between forms of masculinity The other women lawmakers did not contribute to the discussion.	Dr. Garin was the only woman lawmaker who participated in the discussion on the use of the term abortion complications against three male colleagues who advocated for the term post-pregnancy complications.

problems as violence against women, lack of representation and political decision-making or unemployment. (*Minutes of the Meeting of the Committee on Women, Philippine House of Representatives, 27 November 2007*, 2007, pp. 31–32).

In this excerpt, Luistro highlighted their opposition to the use of the term reproductive rights and explained that it means the same as contraception and abortion in various contexts. The minutes of the bicameral conference committee meeting showed the same conflicts. Notably, the contested provisions were those that challenged Catholic doctrines, specifically abortion and pre-marital sexual relations. However, in justifying the inclusion of provisions on providing health services for women suffering from abortion complications, Congressman Edcel Lagman also referred to Christian values. The following excerpt illustrates this:

> Now, this is, the management of abortion complications is a very Christian trait. I would compare this to an incident where police officers or military men would have an encounter with rebels, and one of the rebels was wounded … I think it is the obligation of the agents of the state to bring that rebel to a hospital facility for medical treatment. That act, that Christian act of bringing a wounded rebel to a medical facility is not condoning rebellion. So we strongly believe that the Senate version of the management of abortion complications is not condoning abortion. It is a Christian trait which we should encourage. (*Bicameral Conference Committee on the Disagreeing Provisions of House Bill 4273 and Senate Bill 2396 Re Magna Carta of Women*, 2009, pp. 75–76)

This statement demonstrates how lawmakers refer to Christian values to negotiate the contentious provisions of the bill. Comparing a woman suffering from abortion complications to a wounded rebel accomplished two things. First, it confirmed the Committee's stand that the MCW will not be used to legalize abortion. Hence, women who decide to go through abortion remain to be considered outlaws. Second, it harmonized the provision with the Christian value of compassion while upholding the pre-eminence of Philippine laws against abortion.

One word included in the MCW that remains controversial is the word 'ethical' to describe family planning methods under Section 17 on Women's Right to Health. The insistence on inserting the word *ethical* in the state's provision for family planning methods shows the plea to religious morality following the Philippine Catholic Church's position on the matter to avoid the use of contraceptives (Ruiz Austria, 2004; Tanyag, 2015). The legislators who lobbied to remove the term argued that it is subjective and lay open to various interpretations of those mandated by the state to provide this service. The decision to remove the word 'ethical' was duly recorded in the minutes of the meeting (*Bicameral Conference Committee on the Disagreeing Provisions of House Bill 4273 and Senate Bill 2396 Re Magna Carta of Women*, 2009, pp. 66–67). I found no official document or record that explains how the term 'ethical' reappeared in the version ratified by President Gloria Macapagal-Arroyo.

On the definition of gender

The minutes of the meeting showed that lawmakers consulted a Catholic priest, Archbishop Cruz, on defining the concept of gender (*Bicameral Conference Committee on the Disagreeing Provisions of House Bill 4273 and Senate Bill 2396 Re Magna Carta of Women*, 2009, p. 17). Most male lawmakers expressed apprehension about the internationally accepted definition of the concept. They were leaning towards conflating the concepts of sex and gender. The women members of the Committee, particularly Congresswoman Janet Garin, a medical doctor, and women party-list representatives[6] Liza Maza and Luzviminda Ilagan, disagreed with this proposition. Congresswoman Maza argued that by strictly adhering to the concept of sex, the law could be discriminatory against LGBTQI, to which Senator Pimentel responded: 'This is not the Magna Carta for homosexuals' (*Bicameral Conference Committee on the Disagreeing Provisions of House Bill 4273 and Senate Bill 2396 Re Magna Carta of Women*, 2009, p. 23).

Senator Pimentel's position reflects the norm in Philippine society and culture of the binary conception of gender. This prevailing ideology limits the discussion of gender rights in the socio-political and economic realms. For instance, article 1 of the Family Code of the Philippines defines marriage as 'a special contract of permanent union between a man and a woman entered into in accordance with law for the establishment of conjugal and family life.' Article 2 of the Code specifies that parties 'must be a male and a female'.[7] After a lengthy discussion, the lawmakers agreed not to define the word gender. It was evident in the deliberation that lawmakers opted to avoid the complexity of the issues associated with defining the concept of gender. Instead of opening the conversation to include LGBTQI[8] rights, the legislators decided to define women's rights using the dualistic conception of gender. As argued by Lazar (2007), 'deviations from gender-appropriate norms are policed and contained in the presence of a prevailing discourse of heteronormativity' (p. 148). (Table 2)

On equal access to education

The legislators also debated the provision related to dismissing students and teachers based on pregnancy outside of marriage. The debate focused on whether this provision violates institutions' academic freedom, particularly those affiliated with or under the auspices of religious organizations. Before the MCW, schools had the prerogative to remove students and teachers who become pregnant without being married. (Table 3)

These excerpts illustrate how the male legislators advocating for academic freedom regard pregnancy as women's sole responsibility. They seem unmindful of how women are penalized in this situation. In the case of Struck versus Secretary of Defense, Prof. Ruth Bader-Ginsburg argued that 'pregnancy discrimination is sex discrimination' and that 'women's equality and women's reproductive freedom are inextricably linked' (Siegel & Siegel, 2015, p. 796). The study of Shalev (2000), which examined state parties' periodic reports under CEDAW, reveals that policymakers' attitudes play an important role in addressing women's reproductive rights issues. In the Philippine context, the conflict of gender equality principles, particularly in reproductive health, with Catholic doctrines remains a significant hurdle in legislation addressing these policy issues (Ruiz Austria, 2004; Tanyag, 2015).

Conclusion

The legislative proceedings leading to the passage of the Philippine version of the CEDAW showed the Catholic Church's influence in defining gender norms in the Philippine context. Comparing the CEDAW recommendations with the Magna Carta of Women

Table 2. Analysis of the Discussion on the Definition of Gender using Gender Relationality (Lazar, 2000, 2007).

Gender Relationality's Focus on Two Types of Relationships (Lazar, 2000, 2007)	The Bicameral Conference Committee Meeting on the Contentious Provisions of the Magna Carta of Women
Discursive *co-constructions* of ways of doing and being a woman and a man in particular communities of practice	**On the Definition of 'Gender'**
	The Committee consulted a Catholic priest, Archbishop Cruz, on defining the concept of gender.
Male lawmaker promoting the binary conception of gender	Senator Pimentel (man): *I cannot understand why when we talk of Magna Carta for Women we have to talk of other variations of womanhood* (Laughter).
A Congresswoman advocating for the inclusion of the LGBT	Congresswoman Maza (addressing the Chair): *Indeed when we talk about gender, we don't only talk about men and women. We talk about gays and lesbians as well. And are you saying that we are not accepting lesbians or gays or homosexuals within this definition?*
The Chair of the Committee, a woman Senator, attempting to reconcile the disparate ideas of gender; Highlights the 'spiritual point of view'	Senator Madrigal, Chair of the Committee (woman): *The Chair is coming from a more spiritual point of view in our desire to harmonize the Philippine culture with the WHO definitions, and that is why we put 'nature'.*
Dynamics between forms of masculinity A woman senator promotes the traditional view of femininity but acknowledges that some could consider her idea problematic	Senator Madrigal, Chair of the Committee (woman): *I might be accused of being sexist, but foreign men come to the Philippines because they say Philippine women are still feminine. I think that is a nice attribution to our women. I always believe in gender equality between men and women but not necessarily a homogeneity between them* For this provision, three women lawmakers and one male lawmaker advocated for the WHO and UN definition of gender. In contrast, the rest of the lawmakers were inclined to insert the word nature in the definition, including the Chair of the Senate Committee on Women and the Chair of the Committee on Women at the Lower House (both women).

showed which recommendations were excluded. Using FCDA revealed the dynamics of gender in legislators' discourses and how this shaped the Philippine women's rights law. The male legislators primarily argued against provisions aligned with CEDAW articles and recommendations, conceptualizing gender and discrimination from the traditional perspective advocated by the Catholic Church. The negative depiction of reproductive rights as 'anti-childbearing' and 'tantamount to abortion' prevented the substantial discussion of the impact of punitive measures on women undergoing an abortion. The analysis of the deliberations also showed how women lawmakers were more active in advocating for non-discrimination provisions but had to negotiate with their colleagues to make the contentious provisions more acceptable for all parties. This 'negotiation' led to the omission of the definition of gender and the watering down of reproductive health provisions.

Notes

1. In the Philippine legislative process, in case there are conflicting provisions in the Senate (Upper House) and the House of Representatives (Lower House) versions of the bill, the bicameral conference committee is established to reconcile these differences.
2. The conferees of the bicameral conference committee include one female senator, seven female members of the House of Representatives, two male senators, and three male members of the House of Representatives

Table 3. Analysis of the discussion on the Discrimination Against Women in Educational Institutions using Gender Relationality (Lazar, 2000, 2007).

Gender Relationality's Focus on Two Types of Relationships (Lazar, 2000, 2007)	The Bicameral Conference Committee Meeting on the Contentious Provisions of the Magna Carta of Women
Discursive *co-constructions* of ways of doing and being a woman and a man in particular communities of practice	On Discrimination Against Women in Educational Institutions There was a general agreement among all lawmakers that educational institutions should not dismiss women students and faculty on account of pregnancy outside marriage.
Male lawmaker advocating for the Catholic schools; Depiction of unwed mothers as immoral and unrighteous. Another male lawmaker agrees that employees should 'conform' to the institution's standards. Note how both do not question whether these standards could be inequitable.	*Congressman Zialcita:* But if you're running a Catholic school where you are preaching morality and righteousness, supposing there are 50 of the teachers who are pregnant outside marriage, it becomes very difficult to explain it to the student. *Senator Pimentel (male):* Implicit in that academic freedom is the right to remove people who do not conform to the requirements of a particular school under the circumstances.
A Congresswoman questions the provision and raises the issue of discrimination.	*Congresswoman Garin:* Why don't we include the father? The one who impregnated the teacher or the student?
Male lawmakers conceptualization of pregnancy as a women's sole responsibility; Discussion of discrimination is not taken seriously, or using humor as a deflection strategy. Sexist humor promotes a patriarchal ideology (Bemiller & Schneider, 2010).	*Congressman Zialcita:* This is the Magna Carta for Women, not Magna Carta for Husbands. *Laughter.*
A Congresswoman explains how the male lawmakers' conception of pregnancy leads to the unfair treatment of women Congresswoman Maza's argument brought back the discrimination issue, which was being evaded as the male lawmakers focused on the concept of academic freedom.	*Congresswoman Maza:* I think it is incumbent upon me to manifest based on a feminist perspective why this specific provision is included here. Earlier, it was just laughed upon that the men should not be included because this is not the Magna Carta for Men. That's precisely the problem. Both the man and the woman decided to have sex and enjoyed it, but the woman who gets pregnant gets punished by society. The man gets to stay in the school. That's why we are saying that there are discriminatory practices like this. That's the logic behind this provision.
Dynamics between forms of masculinity Notice how more women lawmakers participated in the discussion to remove the discriminatory provision compared to the abortion and gender provisions.	Five women lawmakers participated in the discussion to support the removal of the discriminatory provision. Two male lawmakers also took the side of the women lawmakers. Based on their arguments, three male lawmakers were inclined to retain the discriminatory provision.

3. The six disagreeing provisions were under Section 2 Declaration of Policy on the principles of human rights of women, specifically on the concept of universal human rights; Section 4 on the Definition of Gender; Section 13 on Equal Access and Elimination of Discrimination in Education, Scholarships, and Training specifically on the dismissal of women from educational institutions on account of pregnancy outside of marriage; Section 15 on Women in Military, where lawmakers decided to expand the provision to include the police and other similar services; Section 17 on Women's Right to Health; specifically the inclusion of the word 'ethical' in the methods of family planning; and Section 19 on Equal Rights in All Matters Relating to Marriage and Family Relations, specifically the use of the concept of common-law relationships.

4. Article II, Section 12 of the 1987 Philippine Constitution states 'The State recognizes the sanctity of family life and shall protect and strengthen the family as a basic autonomous social institution. It shall equally protect the life of the mother and the life of the unborn from conception.' Articles 256–259 of the The Revised Penal Code of the Philippines, Act. No. 3815 penalizes abortion.

5. The Family Code (Executive Order No. 209) is the Philippines' basic law on persons and family relations. In March 2018, during the 17th Congress, the House of Representatives voted for the passage of House Bill 07303 'An Act Instituting Absolute Divorce and Dissolution of Marriage in the Philippines' but there was no counterpart bill in the Senate. Three versions of the bill has been filed in the current 18th Congress both in the House of Representatives and the Senate.
6. To provide representation to marginalised sectors of the society such as the labour, peasant, urban poor, indigenous cultural communities, women, and youth, the Philippine Constitution included a provision for sectoral or party-list representatives constituting 20 per cent of the lower house. Gabriela Women's Party (GWP), managed to obtain seats in in the 13th to 18th Congresses
7. In the case of Falcis III v. Civil Registrar-General (G.R. No. 217910), the Philippine Supreme Court dismissed the petition questioning the constitutionality of these provisions in the Family Code. In its ruling, the Supreme Court stated: 'Lest the exercise of its power amount to a ruling on the wisdom of the policy imposed by Congress on the subject matter of the law, the judiciary does not arrogate unto itself the rule-making prerogative by a swift determination that a rule ought not exist'. Stated simply, the Judiciary leaves the issue on same-sex marriage to the hands of the Legislature.
8. The Philippine House of Representatives passed the Sexual Orientation and Gender Identity Expression (SOGIE) Equality Bill during the 17th Congress (2017). It has been referred to as the non-discrimination bill which prohibits gender-based discrimination. The bill did not have the same support in the Senate. Versions of the bill have been refiled in the 18th Congress.

Disclosure statement

No potential conflict of interest was reported by the author(s).

Funding

This work was supported by The University of Auckland Doctoral Scholarships [No grant number provided].

References

Acharya, A. (2004). How ideas spread: Whose norms matter? Norm localization and institutional change in Asian regionalism. *International Organization*, *58*(2), 239–275. https://doi.org/10.1017/S0020818304582024

Acker, J. (1992). From sex roles to gendered institutions. *Contemporary Sociology*, *21*(5), 565–569. http://www.jstor.org/stable/2075528 https://doi.org/10.2307/2075528

Baldez, L. (2011). The un convention to eliminate all forms of discrimination against women (CEDAW): A new way to measure women's interests. *Politics & Gender*, *7*(3), 419–423. https://doi.org/10.1017/S1743923X11000183

Bemiller, M. L., & Schneider, R. Z. (2010). It's not just a joke. *Sociological Spectrum*, *30*(4), 459–479. https://doi.org/10.1080/02732171003641040

Bicameral Conference Committee on the Disagreeing Provisions of House Bill 4273 and Senate Bill 2396 Re Magna Carta of Women. (2009).

Brandt, M., & Kaplan, J. (1995). The tension between women's rights and religious rights: Reservations to CEDAW by Egypt, Bangladesh and Tunisia. *Journal of Law and Religion, 12*(1), 105–142. https://doi.org/10.2307/1051612

Childs, S. (2013). Negotiating gendered institutions: Women's parliamentary friendships. *Politics & Gender, 9*(2013), 127–151. https://doi.org/10.1017/S1743923X13000019

Curtin, J. (2018). Feminist innovations and New institutionalism. In M. Sawer & K. Baker (Eds.), *Gender innovation in political science. Gender and politics.* (pp. 115–133). Palgrave Macmillan, Cham. https://doi.org/10.1007/978-3-319-75850-3_6

Draude, A. (2017). Translation in motion: A concept's journey towards norm diffusion studies. *Third World Thematics: A TWQ Journal, 2*(5), 588–605. https://doi.org/10.1080/23802014.2017.1436984

Englehart, N. A., & Miller, M. K. (2014). The CEDAW effect: International law's impact on women's rights. *Journal of Human Rights, 13*(1), 22–47. https://doi.org/10.1080/14754835.2013.824274

Kenny, M. (2007). Gender, institutions and power: A critical review. *Politics, 27*(2), 91–100. https://doi.org/10.1111/j.1467-9256.2007.00284.x

Lazar, M. M. (2000). Gender, discourse and semiotics: The politics of parenthood representations. *Discourse & Society, 11*(3), 373–400. https://doi.org/10.1177/0957926500011003005

Lazar, M. M. (2005a). *Feminist critical discourse analysis: Gender, power and ideology in discourse.* Palgrave Macmillan.

Lazar, M. M. (2005b). Politicizing gender in discourse: Feminist critical discourse analysis as political perspective and praxis. *Feminist Critical Discourse Analysis: Gender, Power and Ideology in Discourse*, 1–30. https://doi.org/10.1057/9780230599901

Lazar, M. M. (2007). Feminist critical discourse analysis: Articulating a feminist discourse praxis. *Critical Discourse Studies, 4*(2), 141–164. https://doi.org/10.1080/17405900701464816

Lazar, M. M. (2014). Feminist critical discourse analysis. In S. Ehrlich, M. Meyerhoff, & J. Holmes (Eds.), *The handbook of language, gender, and sexuality* (pp. 180–199). John Wiley & Sons, Ltd. https://doi.org/10.4324/9781315739342

Liebowitz, D. J., & Zwingel, S. (2014). Gender equality oversimplified: Using CEDAW to counter the measurement obsession. *International Studies Review, 16*(3), 362–389. https://doi.org/10.1111/misr.12139

Machin, D., & Mayr, A. (2012). Concealing and taking for granted: Nominalization and presupposition. In *How to do critical discourse analysis* (pp. 137–162).

Mackay, F., Kenny, M., & Chappell, L. (2010). New institutionalism through a gender lens: Towards a feminist institutionalism? *International Political Science Review, 31*(5), 573–588. https://doi.org/10.1177/0192512110388788

Mackay, F., & Waylen, G. (2009). Feminist institutionalism. *Politics & Gender, 5*(02), 237–280. https://doi.org/10.1017/S1743923X09000178

Minto, R., & Mergaert, L. (2018). Gender mainstreaming and evaluation in the EU: Comparative perspectives from feminist institutionalism. *International Feminist Journal of Politics, 20*(2), 204–220. https://doi.org/10.1080/14616742.2018.1440181

Minutes of the Meeting of the Committee on Women, Philippine House of Representatives, 27 November 2007. (2007).

Ruiz Austria, C. S. (2004). The church, the state and women's bodies in the context of religious fundamentalism in the Philippines. *Reproductive Health Matters, 12*(24), 96–103. https://doi.org/10.1016/S0968-8080(04)24152-0

Savery, L. (2007). *Engendering the state: The international diffusion of women's human rights.* Routledge.

Shalev, C. (2000). Rights to sexual and reproductive health: The ICPD and the convention on the Elimination of All Forms of Discrimination against women. *Health and Human Rights, 4*(2), 38–66. http://www.jstor.com/stable/4065196 https://doi.org/10.2307/4065196

Siegel, N. S., & Siegel, R. B. (2015). Struck by stereotype : Ruth bader ginsburg on pregnancy discrimination as sex discrimination. *The Legacy of Ruth Bader Ginsburg, 59*(4), 44–56. https://doi.org/10.1017/CBO9781107477131.006

Tanyag, M. (2015). Unravelling the intersections of power: The case of sexual and reproductive freedom in the Philippines. *Women's Studies International Forum, 53*, 63–72. https://doi.org/10.1016/j.wsif.2015.10.002

Thomson, J. (2018). Resisting gendered change: Feminist institutionalism and critical actors. *International Political Science Review, 39*(2), 178–191. https://doi.org/10.1177/0192512116677844

Weiss, A. M. (2003). Interpreting Islam and Women's Rights: Implementing CEDAW in Pakistan. *International Sociology, 18*(3), 581–601. https://doi.org/10.1177/02685809030183007

Zwingel, S. (2012). How Do norms travel? Theorizing international women's rights in transnational Perspective1. *International Studies Quarterly, 56*(1), 115–129. https://doi.org/10.1111/j.1468-2478.2011.00701.x

Zwingel, S. (2013). Translating international women's rights norms: CEDAW in context. In *Feminist strategies in international governance* (pp. 111–126). https://doi.org/10.4324/9780203094969

Zwingel, S. (2016). *Translating international women's rights: The CEDAW convention in context.* Palgrave Macmillan. https://doi.org/10.1057/978-1-137-31501-4

The depoliticization of law in the news: BBC reporting on US use of extraterritorial or 'long-arm' law against China

Le Cheng, Xiaobin Zhu and David Machin

ABSTRACT
In this paper we explore how a public national media outlet, the British BBC, represents an international legal case which has a highly political nature. The case is US versus Huawei/Meng Wanzhou, which took place between 2018 and 2021. Accusations were that the Chinese technology company committed fraud, leading the global HSBC bank to breach US sanctions against Iran. The charges were made by the US using what is called an 'extraterritorial law', which, while rejected as law by governments around the world, is policed by US economic powers and control over international finance. Using Critical Discourse Analysis we show that, while the BBC presents much detail of legal process, the actual nature of the law the US uses to bring criminal charges against international companies and banks, is neither considered nor questioned. Our interest is how such a law, which has a huge influence over global trade and politics, is presented to the public in this particular case. We contribute to the position that the nature of laws, how they are used and known, must always be understood within the prevailing discourses of the moment.

Introduction

In December 2018 Meng Wanzhou, the chief financial officer of the telecommunications technology company Huawei, was arrested during her transit from China at Vancouver airport. The US Department of Justice issued 23 charges, and called for her extradition from Canada to the US for trial. Specifically, Meng was accused of failing to inform the HSBC bank as to the ownership of an Iranian-based communications company called Skycom by Huawei, leading to investments that would violate US sanctions against Iran. Meng was placed under house arrest. Over the next three years there was a sequence of hearings where Canadian courts had to determine whether the fraud charges also constituted a crime in Canada, a condition required for extradition. After three years, the Canadian court finally rejected extradition when it became clear that the US had no case since the bank already had full knowledge of ownership of the company and had in fact represented both of them for over 15 years. Meng was released in September 2021. During the case, the situation became more complicated as China also held two Canadian citizens, accused them of spying, and put additional pressure on the Canadian government.

The US legal case was based on what is known as 'extraterritorial jurisdiction' or 'long-arm jurisdiction'. This is where laws made in one state are extended to the conduct of persons and organizations of other states and may not involve their consent (Veneziano, 2019: p. 189). The US has a number of these laws such as the *Foreign Corrupt Practices Act* (FCPA) and the *International Emergency Economic Powers Act* (IEEPA). While many countries have such extraterritorial laws, the US has used its own laws more consistently and extensively, taking advantage of its superpower status to enforce them (Efrat, 2022).

Both the FCPA and IEEPA were created to protect US interests around the world, charging penalties to US and foreign companies and persons in relation to terrorism, corruption, tax evasion, and those who deal with countries under US sanctions deemed as US enemies (Banna, 2017; Breen, 2021). Companies found breaking these laws are given fines that may be billions of dollars (Haedicke and Schroeder, 2009, Buchanan and Zabala, 2017). Companies have little choice but to comply, as the US can use its economic power in world finance to impose sanctions, punishments and exclusions (Roche, 2021c), meaning that multinational banks and companies could face disastrous trading restrictions (Terry, 2020).

Such long-arm jurisdiction, it has been argued, can be used as a "political and economic lever to apply US determined standards on non-US entities and citizens or as a means of forcing its international partners to toe the line on US determined policies" (Roche 2021a: 5). Such laws, therefore, "pose a severe threat to both the territorial and economic sovereignty and integrity" of the states upon which they are imposed (Veneziano, 2019:189) – despite being unlawful themselves (Terry 2020). While national governments strive to find ways to push back against these extraterritorial laws, the force available to the US means that they are "more or less helpless" (Lohmann, 2019: 1). As Roche (2021b) notes, writing for the EU: 'The extent to which the US has assumed extraterritorial jurisdiction and its willingness to use that outreach as a political and economic lever is disturbing'.

It has been shown that laws, legal processes and legal decision making do not exist as a form of some kind of rational code external to, or above, society, which is how they are often represented (Cotterrell, 1984). Rather, laws are shaped by prevailing discourses of the time, which lay out what can be thought of as acceptable and reasonable accounts of events in the world (Jessup and Rubenstein, 2012; Dryzek, 2007; Gruber, 2017). The laws, legal claims and decision-making that lay out kinds of agents, responsibilities, causes and logic, are shaped by the prevailing, and shifting, discursive frames of different times (Ashton and Aydos, 2019).

In this paper our aim is neither to assess the nature of extraterritorial laws per se, nor to ask whether they are appropriately applied in the Meng case. Drawing on Van Leeuwen (2008) we draw out the 'discursive script', used by the BBC to represent the legal case over a sequence of 28 news reports from 2018 to 2021, as the case began, progressed and concluded. The notion of 'discursive script' describes how the goings-on of an event are represented in language – what kinds of participants, actions, settings, causalities and ideas are involved. For Van Leeuwen (2008), it is useful to ask if, or how, a discursive script *recontextualizes* an actual concrete set of events, so that some of these elements are somehow different, missing, with new ones added, or sequentially changed.

Our analysis shows that the BBC discursive script aligns with the discourse carried by the legal case presented by the US Department of Justice. The legitimacy of the long-arm law is not questioned and the actual charges, which are somewhat obfuscated, merge with a discourse prevalent at the time that China was a threat to Western systems and values.

We spend the first part of the paper accounting for the actual setting and nature of the events that comprise the Meng case. This allows us to then draw out the discursive script and recontextualizations used to represent them by the BBC.

The context of the trade war

The Meng case can be understood as one part of the ongoing trade war between the US and China and in particular about US anxieties over China's rapid growth (Sukar and Ahmed, 2019). More recently, US concerns have been driven by the US trade deficit with China, resulting in policies of the Trump administration in 2018 and 2019 including imposition of new heavy trade tariffs (Li, Balistreri and Zhang, 2019).

One key part of this trade war had been the matter of technology, particularly in relation to communications and information (Chen, Chen and Dondeti, 2020). Trump had begun the issue of national security in relation to China, supported by industry lobbyists, in reference to steel and aluminum in 2018, but this was soon to include technology, information and intellectual property (Steinbock, 2018). One key concern had been Huawei overtaking Apple and Samsung as world leader in mobile and equipment sales (Canals and Singla, 2020).

Both Trump and later Biden added major Chinese tech companies such as ZTE and Huawei to what is called the 'US Entity List', which contains persons, companies and institutions seen as a threat to American national security. This would make it difficult for these companies operating in the US to work with domestic institutions, restrict the issue of operating licenses from regulators, and prevent them from buying up US companies (Shepardson, 2021) and in 2020 the US passed a law to heighten controls over any Chinese company listed on the stock market (Canals and Singla, 2020).

The issue of national security was based on accusations of intellectual theft and spying first brought by Trump, which has been seen by many as simply a symptom of an established power feeling threatened by a rising rival (Allison, 2017). It was argued that these accusations had little concrete evidence and were simply part of a strategy to damage, or slow the rise of Chinese technology companies (Agnel and Mayeda, 2017). As Steinbock (2018) observes, the very commission created by Trump to carry out the investigations into Chinese tech companies was comprised of Trump associates, former US military, and senators associated with anti-communism. The US passed a number of domestic laws to limit the operations of Chinese companies (Shepardson, 2021) and also began to put pressure on its allies around the world to do the same (Lohmann, 2019, The Economist, 2019).

The Meng/Huawei case

The nature of the US case against Meng must be placed in the context of an earlier use of long-arm jurisdiction by the US against the HSBC bank. In December 2012, HSBC paid the

US $1.92 billion and entered into a 5-year Deferred Prosecution Agreement (DPA) for money laundering and transactions with sanctioned countries, which included Iran. HSBC had been charged with violating the long-arm IEEPA and Trading with the Enemy Act (TWEA). It committed to cooperate with the US DOJ in any further investigations (Department of Justice, 2012). It was later in 2016 that the US DOJ requested all information on Huawei. In return, further potential charges against HSBC were waived (Lewis, 2021). As the Canadian judge at the extradition hearing noted, it could just as easily have been HSBC facing the charges of dealing with Iran (Lewis, 2021).

The details of the charges against Meng were that in 2013 she had misled the HSBC bank over the nature of Huawei's relationship with Hong Kong-based telecommunications company Skycom (Freifield and Stecklow, 2019). Skycom had formerly been directly owned by Huawei and had carried out operations in Iran. While this ownership had been since severed, links between the two companies were still strong (Liu, 2021). During a meeting with HSBC, Meng is said to have displayed a PowerPoint presentation that excluded this information. By not disclosing this information, it was argued, HSBC had been led into violating US sanctions against Iran (Yates, 2021). It was the violation of US sanctions against Iran that was foregrounded as a main factor motivating the request of the US to Canada to arrest and extradite Meng (Ruyt, 2019). The court hearings in Vancouver were to establish if this also constituted a criminal act in Canada, in which case the US request for extradition would be carried out.

According to the Secretary of the US Department of Homeland Security, Meng, as CFO of Huawei, had conducted millions of dollars in transactions that were in direct violation of the Iranian Transactions and Sanctions Regulations (ITSR), which would come under the International Emergency Economic Powers Act (IEEPA). IEEPA, passed by US Congress in 1977 is the foundation of the modern US sanctions regime (Meagher, 2020).

The IEEPA is used by the US government to enforce sanctions on persons or entities that have no territorial or personal connection with America and would not normally be subject to American law (Breen, 2021). The Iranian Transactions and Sanctions Regulations, therefore, apply to any person evading restrictions in relation to Iran (Rennack, 2018). The IEEPA has caused problems for companies and banks around the world that have established relationships with Iran, where a turnaround in US policy can quickly result in fines of up to billions of dollars unless they cease business activities with the sanctioned country (Lohmann, 2019; The Economist, 2019). In Europe, there have been attempts to protect EU existing financial interests but these attempts have had little effect, simply due to the massive consequences of being excluded from major world financial routes dominated by the US (Roche, 2021b).

The Meng case progressed until the end of 2021 as prosecutors in Canada assessed whether indeed Meng should be extradited to the US for trial. This did not involve an assessment of her guilt, only of whether the charges could be characterized as criminal in Canada. This is called the requirement of 'double criminality' (Vikander and Warburton, 2020).

The most significant court hearings took place in July and August 2020 where Meng's lawyers pushed for the release of documents from HSBC, which showed that the bank was aware of the relationship between Huawei and Skycom, since the bank had represented both for 15 years (Warburton, 2020). The Canadian judge denied use of the documents, as the issue was not about trying the case per se, only to establish if the charges qualify under Canadian law. However, the documents, obtained by Meng's lawyers, were strategically released into the public domain in 2021 (Lewis, 2021).

In August 2021, in light of public knowledge of the documents, the judge presiding over the proceedings described Meng's case as highly "unusual" since it is uncommon to see a fraud case with no actual harm many years later (Wintour, 2021). It was also questionable that HSBC could be presented as a victim in a fraud case, especially since it appeared to have had all the facts, had a 15-year working relationship with Huawei and Skycom, and as a multinational bank would be unlikely to act on the information of a single person and on the basis of one PowerPoint presentation (Lewis, 2021). The US withdrew its request for extradition. Meng reached what is called a Deferred Prosecution Agreement (DPA) with US prosecutors to end the fraud case against her (AJIL 2022). The DPA meant all charges would be dropped providing Meng admitted to making untrue statements about Huawei's business in Iran. This allowed the US to publicly claim some kind of victory through the admission (Lewis, 2021).

In what follows we draw out the discursive script used by the BBC to represent this case over the 3 years. We cannot here do justice to all the aspects of the reporting we would like to include. But we can reveal the basis of the script, of its participants, their actions, the setting, and causalities.

Methodology

Critical Discourse Analysis is concerned with the function of language in social and political life. The assumption is that language choices are never neutral but shape how the world, things, processes, events and persons are represented (Flowerdew and Richardson, 2017). And such, representations can favor certain interests over others. These things can be selectively represented, shaped, or what Van Leeuwen (2008) would call 'recontextualized' in ways that are ideologically based.

The concept of 'discourse,' drawing on Foucault (1972), is central to CDA. Discourses can be thought of as models of the world and how things work. Importantly, choices in language, to represent a person or process for example, can signify a certain model of the world that may not be openly expressed.

Discourses are comprised of what Van Leeuwen (2008) calls 'discursive scripts.' These are made up of elements such as identities, ideas, values, settings, times, causalities, evaluations, etc. (Van Leeuwen, 2008). Recontextualization is where accounts of processes and events change some of these elements, or where elements are removed. Causalities may be reversed, replaced, or made unclear. Elements may be brought into the foreground and made salient. Other important elements may be pushed into the background or excluded. All such recontextualization is ideologically motivated. In this paper, our interest is in revealing the discursive script communicated by the BBC, drawing out where recontextualization of the events, actors and situations described above has taken place.

It has been well established that versions of the world carried in news media are shaped largely by leading institutions and organizations who form the routine sources for journalists (Schlesinger and Tumber, 1994). As Fairclough (1995) notes, the discourses found in news reports are therefore based already on the recontextualizations produced by the documents and statements fashioned by these sources, which will reflect their aims, values and priorities. What we show in this paper is how the BBC carry the recontextualizations of the main sources used for these reports, which are largely from the US Department of Justice, then adding other material and other layers of recontextualization that align with the discursive script that this communicates. What we are able to show is how the nature and legitimacy of the US long-arm law, used against Huawei and routinely against other countries around the world (Dryzek, 2007), must be understood in the context of wider notions about legality present in dominant discourses carried in relation to particular domains in specific places at certain times.

We begin by looking at how the BBC represents the charges against Huawei and Meng. We then look at how details of legal processes are used to bring a sense of deeper reporting and insights, substituting actual analysis. We then consider how the BBC evaluates the intentions of the Chinese and US participants.

The representation of the charges against Meng

At the heart of this discursive script is the nature of the crime of which Meng is accused.
In the first BBC report on December 6th we find this represented in the following manner:
Extract 1:

> Although it's still not clear what the charges against her are - we know that the US has been investigating Huawei for possible violations of US sanctions on Iran – this is not simply a case about the arrest of one woman, or just one company.

We see here that it is stated that the charges are 'still not clear'. The BBC acknowledges it is unable to say exactly why Meng is being held. But the language used is important. Despite the lack of clarity, there is nevertheless a sense of 'bringing facts' to the reader. We find this with the use of the high modality 'we know' to suggest something established in regard to the investigation of violations of US sanctions on Iran. We find the indicative mood throughout to present information confidently, as certain as in 'this is not simply a case about the arrest of one woman, or just one company'.

Whether the 'investigations' are legitimate or politically motivated is not considered. And the agent of the 'investigating', driven by the Trump elected panel, is here glossed over as 'the US'. Missing from the discursive script, therefore, is the notion that the arrest may be part of the same process as the investigations – both aspects of the US strategy to delegitimize Huawei.

Notably here, the nature of the long-arm jurisdiction the US is using to bring charges is neither raised nor questioned. It is taken as given that the US has the legal power to investigate and press charges where other countries around the world do not obey its sanctions. This continues throughout reporting of the case over the coming years and forms a central part of the discursive script. Absent from this script are the struggles undergone by governments around the world as US policy shifts and national companies, banks and investments are thrown into turmoil.

Over the following days, reports include a little more information. Notable here is how motives and agency are attributed to Meng.
Extract 2:

> On Friday, the Supreme Court of British Columbia was told that Ms Meng had *used* a Huawei subsidiary called Skycom to *evade* sanctions on Iran between 2009 and 2014. (December 8 2018)

Extract 3:

Prosecutors say she *conspired* to defraud banks by *telling* banks a Huawei subsidiary was a separate company – thereby *helping* Huawei circumvent US trade bans.

US prosecutors say Ms Meng had publicly *misrepresented* Skycom as being a separate company from Huawei in order *to avoid* sanctions on Iran. It is also alleged she *deceived* banks about the true relationship between the two companies. (December 12 2018)

While the actual details of the case are not yet given and certainly the nature of the long-arm jurisdiction is absent from the script, there is a clear sense of the agency of Meng. The verbs *used, evade, avoid, conspired, misrepresented, deceived,* there present a strong sense of Meng's active and deliberate role in these criminal events.

As we saw earlier, many governments seek to support, and even demand, that national companies and banks resist following US sanctions due to economic costs, even if US power makes this hard to do (Lohmann, 2019). As such, this could have been presented very differently in language as a company seeking to *maintain* business operations in the face of US attempts to create leverage through sanctions or to *resist* or *defy* sanctions.

In the DOJ press releases and in the actual charges made against Meng, there were also broader charges that included Huawei more generally in the context of breaches of IEEPA long-arm law, 23 in total. These are reflected in the BBC reports.

Extract 4:

'US lawmakers have <u>repeatedly</u> accused the company of being a threat to US national security, arguing that its technology could be used for spying by the Chinese government'. (2018.12.08)

Extract 5:

US National Security Adviser John Bolton said his country has had "<u>enormous concerns for years</u>" about the practice of Chinese firms "to use stolen American intellectual property, to engage in forced technology transfers, and to be used as arms of the Chinese government's objectives in terms of information technology in particular". (2018.12.9)

No clear link is made between the threat to national security, spying and the Meng case. There is the sense that any investigations by the US in regard to Huawei are likely to be warranted. This obfuscation of the actual charges against Meng continues throughout the BBC coverage.

In fact, none of these broader charges were considered in the extradition case, which was based only on the matter of whether the fraud of which Meng was charged leading a bank to breach sanctions against Iran would also be considered a crime in Canada.

Also important in these extracts is how the US represents the case as an ongoing, repeating problem. In extracts 4 and 5 we see the hedging terms 'repeatedly' and 'for years' used to represent the accusations made by the US. These BBC reports place this event in a discourse where the Chinese government is an ongoing threat to US national security, of which Meng is a part. One aspect of this we do not have the space to address here is the insertion of hyperlinks between paragraphs to other BBC stories about other threats presented by China.

The foregrounding of legal processes

While the nature of the long-arm jurisdiction being used to make these charges is never questioned and the confusion created by the obfuscated nature of the charges brought against Huawei and Meng are not interrogated, there is nevertheless a sense of giving deeper insights into the case. This is done by foregrounding legal processes and legal language. Such information is taken from court reports and US Department of Justice press releases.

We see this in the following extracts:

Extract 6

Ms Meng, 47, will next appear in court on Wednesday, when it will be confirmed that Canada has *issued a legal writ over her extradition* to the US. A date for an extradition hearing will be set.

But this is still the early stages. A judge must *authorize her committal for extradition* and the justice minister would then decide whether to surrender her to the US.

There will be *chances for appeal* and some cases have dragged on for years. (2019.3.4)

Extract 7

The judge must be satisfied that it meets *the so-called "double criminality" test* before agreeing to an extradition. (2021.1.21)

Extract 8

Ms Meng's lawyers launched *a multi-pronged attack* on the US extradition request itself. (2021.9.24).

Much of the language in the BBC reports summarizes or paraphrases the DOJ documents and court proceedings. As we see, some elements are retained. First, we find legal lexis. Here it is connoted that we are given access to the deeper technical details of the case.

In extracts 6-8 we find:

Issued a legal writ

Committal for extradition

Appeal

Double criminality test

Lawyers launched a multi-pronged attack

This foregrounding gives a sense of expert insights into the finer details of the case. Yet this substitutes the lack of the same kind of attention to the law that allows the US to do this in the first place and how such long-arm laws play out across the international community.

There is also a foregrounding of the stages and sequentiality of how the extradition case will play out. In extracts 6-8 we find:

will next appear in court

when it will be confirmed

would then decide

There will be chances for appeal

before agreeing to an extradition

This attention to sequentiality suggests access to the mechanics of the legal case, explaining how things work in the legal process. In the discursive script, this substitutes the larger sequentiality of events in relation to the original use of the long-arm law against HSBC, and the start of the Trump regime's attempts to delegitimize and block Chinese industry in general and technology companies in particular.

The use of artists' sketches of Meng in her court appearances also connote insights into the legal proceedings in the courtroom through familiar iconography. The sketch here, along with the legalese and sequentiality, helps to place these events into a familiar script where the rational process of the law is at work.

The states of mind of the US and China

Discursive scripts include actions and processes. These are the doings of the discourse. Van Leeuwen (2008) notes the importance here of mental processes, namely how verb processes directly or indirectly give access to motivations, feelings and attitudes. These can provide evaluations of the identities and motivations of participants. The verb process representing the US can be categorized into three groups.

The US is worried
First, there are worries and fears about China and Huawei:
Extract 9

But the US and other Western nations *have been concerned* that the Chinese government could use Huawei's technology to expand its spying ability. (2019.1.29)

Extract 10

Some Western governments *fear* Beijing will gain access to fifth-generation (5G) mobile and other communications networks through Huawei and expand its spying ability. (2018.12.6)

The US and the hedged 'Some Western governments' or 'other Western nations' are represented as being concerned, fearful and worried about China. We do not find corresponding states of mind for China, which could have been represented as being *fearful* of the effects of US sanctions, or *concerned* about the use of extraterritorial law to pressure governments around the world.

The US is reasonable
Extract 11

The charges remain unknown but the US *has been probing* Huawei over possible violation of sanctions against Iran.

Other Chinese tech companies with operations in the US, such as social media company TikTok, are also *facing scrutiny*. (2021.9.25)

The US is represented as acting in reasonable, systematic ways that suggest official procedures. So, as we saw in extract 1, the Americans are '*investigating* Huawei'. Here above we see they are *'probing'* and *'scrutinizing'*. These verb processes substitute for the more brutal and arbitrary way that the US uses its power to put pressure on companies, banks and governments around the world to follow its own interests. Again, China is not represented as carrying out any such systematic, official or reasonable procedures. We find no sense of Chinese investigations, probing or other official procedures to put US economic strategies under scrutiny.

The US is determined
Extract 12

The US has <u>not shied away</u> from throwing its weight around to *prevent* the Chinese telecoms giant from being involved in other countries' creations of the high-speed internet networks. (2020.5.27)

Extract 13

Although there are some waivers, US Treasury Secretary Steven Mnuchin has said the US will "<u>*aggressively*" target</u> any firm or organization "evading our sanctions". (2018.12.8)

The US is represented as confronting a problem. It has <u>not shied away</u> from preventing Huawei from being involved in the high-speed networks of other countries. The US here themselves have opted for this representation of an uncompromising approach, for example to *'aggressively' target'*. There is a sense that the US is taking a noble stand rather than in the routing process of dictating the global economy in its own interests.

China is represented through different verb processes:

China as confrontational
Extract 15

The arrest of such a high-profile business figure led to <u>*anger*</u> in China. (2021.9.24)

Extract 16

China *is angry* at her detention, saying she has not violated any laws. (2018.12.18)

The arrest of Ms Meng, the daughter of Huawei's founder, <u>*infuriated*</u> China. (2019.1.29)

Extract 17

China <u>*is demanding*</u> the release of telecoms giant Huawei's chief financial officer, who has been detained in Canada. (2018.12.6)

The mental process of anger and being infuriated is favored for the representation of China. This is done in a personified form. We find no Chinese officials represented as personally saying 'I am angered', nor this being attributed to a single official who states that aggressive action will be taken. In contrast we do not find the US being represented as angry as a whole, nor possessing a single state of mind.

China is also attributed verb processes of not compromising, such as 'demanding' and 'attacking'. But this does not appear as noble as the assertiveness of the US, as again this sits alongside anger and not fears, and rational probes and investigations.

China in denial
Extract 18

In a statement, Huawei *rejected the charges*, saying it didn't commit "any of the asserted violations" and that it "*is not aware*" of any wrongdoing by Ms Meng". (29 January 2019)

Extract 19

China, which *insists* that Ms Meng has not violated any laws, had *threatened* severe consequences unless Canada released the Huawei executive. (2018.12.12)

We are told that China and Huawei deny and reject the charges and are unaware of any wrongdoing, *insisting* that they know nothing of violations. In contrast, we never hear the US *denying* that this case is political, nor *insisting* that the long-arm jurisdiction backed with sanctions, or the pressurizing of governments to block Huawei, is unproblematic.

Conclusion

The analysis in this paper only begins to reveal the elements that comprise the discursive script carried by the BBC coverage. Much more could be said. But we have been able to show how this is a script where the actual nature of US long-arm laws is missing. We are given a compelling case of deep reporting into legal details. But this substitutes actual details of what is taking place legally. The use of the long-arm law, the economic and political power and dominance of the US around the world appears as given and natural in this discursive script. There is no reason to question why the US should have the right to legally control how a foreign bank does business, nor why all countries should follow the sanctions it imposes, creating chaos in their own economies. We might say that this omission would likely be the case, given the BBC reliance on US sources. But the BBC discursive script representing this case is clearly placed in a broader discourse about China as a threat.

What we wanted to show through this analysis is how the nature of any law or legal process cannot be understood outside of the wider hegemonic discourses held in society at any point in time. Law is not external to, or above, society, but is infused into culture, ideas, values and power of time and place. In this case, the economic and political power and dominance of the US around the world appears as given, natural. The US' struggles to delegitimize growing economic threats to its former dominance can be passed off as dealing with a China that is uncompromising, aggressive, and acts outside of acceptable international norms of practice – for which presumably the US is the role model.

This same kind of invisibility or presumed naturalness, we would argue, is true of many of the laws that hover in the background of news reporting, in relation to different kinds of freedoms, health, migration, sustainability, civil rights and many other things. In Critical Discourse Studies we have tended to look at texts that deal with these kinds of domains more broadly, but not in the sense of the laws that underpin them, which like all laws, are infused with the dominant discourses of their time.

One final reflection on the Meng case is that it was well created and managed by the US and the Trump regime. In the end Meng was released, but news outlets around the world publicized the obfuscated charges against her and, like the BBC, carried this discursive script of China as a threat and the US as defenders of global economic order. News outlets became one tool in the US campaign to block China and protect their own waning power.

Disclosure statement

No potential conflict of interest was reported by the author(s).

ORCID

Le Cheng ⓘ http://orcid.org/0000-0002-4423-8585

References

Agnel, P., & Mayeda, A. (2017). "Trump Is Warned His Intellectual-Property Probe Risks a Trade War with China," Bloomberg, October 11, 2017.

AJIL. (2022). Huawei's Meng Wanzhou Released to China after entering into deferred Prosecution agreement with U.S. Justice Department. *American Journal of International Law*, *116*(1), 184–189. https://doi.org/10.1017/ajil.2021.72

Allison, G. (2017). *Destined for war: Can America and China escape Thucydides's trap?* Houghton Mifflin Harcourt.

Ashton, S., & Aydos, E. (2019). Environmental discourses and water law: A case study of the regulation of the Murray-Darling basin. *Sequência (Florianópolis)*, *83*, 47–86. https://doi.org/10.5007/2177-7055.2019v41n83p47

Banna, M. A. (2017). The long arm of US jurisdiction and international law: Extraterritoriality against sovereignty. *Journal of Law, Policy and Globalization*, *60*, 59–70.

Breen, E. (2021). Corporations and US economic sanctions: The dangers of overcompliance. In C. Beaucillon (Ed.), *Research Handbook on unilateral and Extraterritorial sanctions* (pp. 256–269). Edward Elgar Publishing.

Buchanan, B. G., & Zabala, C. A. (2017). Money laundering and legal compliance in the U.S. financial services industry: The case of standard Chartered bank. In M. S. Aßländer, & S. Hudson (Eds.), *The Handbook of business and Corruption* (pp. 255–278). Emerald Publishing Limited.

Canals, C., & Singla, J. (2020). The US-China technology conflict: an initial insight, https://www.caixabankresearch.com/en/node/8906/printable/print

Chen, A. W., Chen, J., & Dondeti, V. R. (2020). The US-China trade war: Dominance of trade or technology? *Applied Economics Letters*, *27*(11), 904–909. https://doi.org/10.1080/13504851.2019.1646860

Cotterrell, R. (1984). *The sociology of law: An introduction*. Oxford: Oxford University Press.

Department of Justice. (2012). HSBC Holdings Plc. and HSBC Bank USA N.A. Admit to Anti-Money Laundering and Sanctions Violations, Forfeit $1.256 Billion in Deferred Prosecution Agreement. https://www.justice.gov/opa/pr/hsbc-holdings-plc-and-hsbc-bank-usa-na-admit-anti-money-laundering-and-sanctions-violations

Dryzek, J. (2007). Paradigms and Discourses. In D. Bodansky, J. Brunée, & E. Hey (Eds.), *The Oxford handbook of international Environmental law* (pp. 1–15). Oxford University Press.

The Economist. (2019). How the American takeover of a French national champion became intertwined in a corruption investigation, https://www.economist.com/business/2019/01/17/how-the-american-takeover-of-a-french-national-champion-became-intertwined-in-a-corruption-investigation

Efrat, A. (2022). Facing US extraterritorial pressure: American troops in foreign courts during the Cold War. *Journal of Politics*, 84(1), 242–257. https://doi.org/10.1086/715254

Fairclough, N. (1995). *Media discourse*. London: Arnold.

Flowerdew, J., & Richardson, J. (2017). *The Routledge Handbook of critical Discourse studies*. Taylor & Francis.

Foucault, M. (1972). *The Archaeology of knowledge*. Routledge.

Freifield, K., & Stecklow, S. (2019). Exclusive: HSBC probe helped lead to U.S. charges against Huawei CFO. https://www.reuters.com/article/cbusiness-us-huawei-hsbc-exclusive-idCAKCN1QF1IA-OCABS

Gruber, S. (2017). The Tension between rights and Cultural heritage Protection in China. In A. Durbach, & L. Lixinski (Eds.), *Heritage, culture and Rights: Challenging legal Discourses* (pp. 149–163). Bloomsbury.

Haedicke, S. J., & Schroeder, M. R. (2009). Foreign Corrupt Practices Act: two recent cases set new records for penalties, teach old lessons, Jones & Walker, ebulletin Corporate Compliance. https://www.joneswalker.com/images/content/8/3/v2/834/1375.pdf

Jessup, B., & Rubenstein, K. (2012). Introduction: Using discourse theory to untangle public and international environmental law. In B. Jessup & K. Rubenstein (Eds.), *Environmental discourses in Public and international Law* (pp. 1–26). Cambridge University Press.

Lewis, R. (2021). Who Is the Winner in the Deal between Meng Wanzhou and the DOJ? Under the Deferred Prosecution Agreement, the DOJ Can Claim that Meng Admitted "Wrong-doing," But All Charges Against Her Can Now Be Dismissed by December 2022. https://www.lexology.com/library/detail.aspx?g=df2a7f76-c7b7-41ba-a1d1-4e9f709443cf

Li, M., Balistreri, E. J., & Zhang, W. (2019). The U.S.-China trade war: Tariff data and general equilibrium analysis. *CARD Working Papers*, 600, 1-18.

Liu, G. (2021). Analysis of Legal Issues Involved in the Meng Wanzhou Case, Asia Law Portal, August 18. https://asialawportal.com/2021/08/18/analysis-of-legal-issues-involved-in-the-meng-wanzhou-case/

Lohmann, S. (2019). Extraterritorial U.S. sanctions: only domestic courts could effectively curb the enforcement of U.S. law abroad. (SWP Comment, 5/2019). Stiftung Wissenschaft und Politik -SWP- Deutsches Institut für Internationale Politik und Sicherheit. https://doi.org/10.18449/2019C05

Meagher, D. (2020). Caught in the economic crosshairs: Secondary sanctions and the American sanctions regime. *Fordham Law Review*, 89(3), 999–1030.

Rennack, D. E. (2018). Iran: U.S. economic sanctions and the authority to lift restrictions. *Current Politics and Economics of the Middle East*, 9, 19–82.

Roche, D. (2021a). Extraterritorial legal outreach: Why should the US call the shots? https://www.euractiv.com/section/global-europe/opinion/extraterritorial-legal-outreach-why-should-the-us-call-the-shots/

Roche, D. (2021b). EU strengthens protection against economic coercion. https://ec.europa.eu/commission/presscorner/detail/en/ip_21_6642?utm_source=dlvr.it&utm_medium=twitter

Roche, D. (2021c) How U.S. extraterritorial legal action affects European companies. Brussels Report. September. https://www.brusselsreport.eu/2021/12/16/how-u-s-extraterritorial-legal-action-affects-european-companies/

Ruyt, J. D. (2019). American sanctions and European sovereignty. *European Policy Brief*, 54, 1–4.

Schlesinger, P., & Tumber, H. (1994). *Reporting Crime: The media Politics of criminal Justice*. Clarendon Press.

Shepardson, D. (2021). Biden signs legislation to tighten U.S. restrictions on Huawei, ZTE. Reuters. https://www.reuters.com/technology/biden-signs-legislation-tighten-us-restrictions-huawei-zte-2021-11-11/

Steinbock, D. (2018). U.S.-China trade war and its global impacts. *China Quarterly of International Strategic Studies*, *4*(4), 515–542. https://doi.org/10.1142/S2377740018500318

Sukar, A., & Ahmed, S. (2019). Rise of trade protectionism: The case of US-Sino trade war. *Transnational Corporations Review*, *11*(4), 279–289. https://doi.org/10.1080/19186444.2019.1684133

Van Leeuwen, T. (2008). *Discourse and Practice: New tools for Critical discourse Analysis*. Oxford University Press.

Veneziano, A. (2019). Extraterritoriality and the regulatory power of the United States: Featured issues of sovereignty, legitimacy, accountability, and democracy. *University of Baltimore Journal of International Law*, *6*(2), 189–214.

Vikander, T., & Warburton, M. (2020). Huawei CFO's lawyer attacks U.S. extradition case in Canadian trial. Reuters. January 20. https://www.reuters.com/article/us-usa-huawei-tech-canada-idUSKBN1ZJ1AN

Warburton, M. (2020). Huawei's Meng back in Canada court as lawyers fight bid to extradite her to U.S. https://www.reuters.com/article/usa-huawei-tech-canada-idUSKBN26J10W

Wintour, P. (2021). Canada, China and US were all doomed to lose in Meng Wanzhou's case. https://www.theguardian.com/technology/2021/sep/24/meng-wanzhou-canada-china-us-settlement-analysis

Yates, S. D. (2021). Will the Canadian Courts make Meng Wanzhou's case their own Lotus? *Scholars International Journal of Law, Crime and Justice*, *4*(3), 136–143. https://doi.org/10.36348/sijlcj.2021.v04i03.002

Is this discursive *Yentling?* A critical study of an RCMP officer's interaction with a child sexual assault complainant

Christopher A. Smith

ABSTRACT

The present study features an interview between a Royal Canadian Mounted Police (RCMP) officer and a female indigenous minor, who was reporting her own sexual assault. The study highlights how the child's interview with the officer appears to include gender-specific judgements. Thus far, few critical studies, underscoring interview techniques, feature power relations and ideologies in the discourse. This study identifies police negotiation with female assault complainants as discursive Yentling. Inspired by the term *Yentl syndrome*, where female health is often underappreciated because it is judged from male prerogatives, the present study proposes that discursive Yentling emerges from victim blaming, perpetrator mitigation, and the sexualization of rape. Drawing attention to transcripts of an RCMP interview with a child complainant, this study asks (1) what power relations and ideologies manifest in the dialogue between the officer and the complainant? (2) Do the findings give evidence for discursive Yentling? Transitivity analysis and a discourse historical approach reveal ideological predispositions towards the complainant during the interview. The implications for this study hopefully provoke more considered police interview techniques for potential victims of sexual assault and inculcate a culture of feminist understanding in Canadian public services.

Introduction

The present study features an interview between a Royal Canadian Mounted Police (RCMP) officer and a female, Indigenous child, who was reporting her own sexual assault in British Columbia, Canada, in 2015. Since 2004, nearly 750,000 sexual assault victims have self-reported in Canada and that number appears to be rising (Conroy & Cotter, 2017). Ideological undercurrents in the discourse underscore a lack of clarity in police interview techniques and may have further traumatized the alleged victim (Haworth, 2017; Venema, 2016). The exchange between the RCMP officer and the child positions the former as a judge of the legitimacy of the alleged assault, so the power relations between them are severely imbalanced (MacLeod, 2010). The officer completely controls the trajectory of the dialogue and reveals hints of a culture of skepticism that resonates with a kind of discursive *Yentling*. Inspired by the term 'Yentl syndrome' (Healy,

1991), where female health is often under-appreciated because it is judged from male prerogatives, discursive Yentling facilitates the diminishment of a female, sexual assault complainant's agency and validity under the pressure of a particular ideology of skepticism and dismissiveness (Greeson et al., 2014) in Canadian police services. This investigation corroborates other studies (Haworth, 2017; Palmater, 2016) that claim a culture of skepticism towards victims of sexual assault are rooted the discourse of police services.

Informed by critical discourse studies (CDS), interview transcripts of the exchange between the RCMP officer and the child, sexual assault complainant are examined for ideologies and power relations in the discourse. Collectively, the findings form a latticework of discursive Yentling, where the child is denied agency unless, as revealed in a similar case in Greeson et al. (2014), she acquiesces to partial responsibility and submits to the RCMP officer's dismissive predisposition.

A Canadian crisis

From 2004, there has been a crisis in the high number of Canadian women and girls, who have been murdered, disappeared or subject to violent, sexualized assault (Conroy & Cotter, 2017; Palmater, 2016; Razack, 2016). The latter of these crimes is underscored in the present study because Indigenous women and girls in Canada are only 2% of the population, but they represent 16% of Canadian female rape victims nationwide (Conroy & Cotter, 2017).

The alleged assault featured in this study did not involve a weapon but is being reported to the RCMP by a child. According to Canada's criminal justice code, the penalty for sexual assault on a minor has a mandatory minimum sentence of one year in jail and a maximum of 16 years (https://laws-lois.justice.gc.ca/). The liability of the RCMP officer featured in the present study depends on the findings of an external review committee who determine if professional misconduct or criminal action occurred during the interview (CACP, 2019).

Although there is a suggestion of intersectionality of race and gender as part of the focus of this study, we underscore the latter because Police services in many Canadian jurisdictions have been accused of victim blaming and lessening perpetrator responsibility, which may have partially enabled a continuation of sexual assaults on women.

A critical look at police interviews

Police officers are uniquely compelled in their duties to interview an alleged victim, then follow-up with more investigation if the incident is deemed worthy to bring before a prosecutorial body (Venema, 2016). However, research suggests that *deeming an incident worthy* is a problematic judgement, overshadowed by management pressures to be *selective* (Palmater, 2016). Atkinson and Drew (1979) characterized police interviews as *minicourtrooms* because the interviewer is an institutional representative who controls exchange and judges the legitimacy of the interviewee, who parleys for credibility (MacLeod, 2010).

The process for complainants who report sexual assault can be distressing, depending on the way it is received (McMillan & Thomas, 2009). For example, engaging with a female officer has been shown to be comforting, while interviews with male officers constitute a secondary trauma (Venema, 2016) because the latter's tendency to be indifferent can be distressing (McMillan & Thomas, 2009). Victims fear to report sexualized assaults because of the very real possibility that they become publicly shamed and re-traumatized in the aftermath (Rich & Seffrin, 2012).

In Canadian Police Services, Venema (2016) discovered a culture of standardized perceptions of sexual assault victims that influence their approach to interviews with female complainants. Rape myths, manifested in assumptions about the victim-offender relationship, weapon involvement, injury, location, etc. (Brownmiller, 1975; Chen & Ullman, 2010; Starzynski et al., 2007; Venema, 2019), pervade police culture in Canada and diminish the credibility of complainants because they inform about an over-estimation of false reporting (Powell & Cauchi, 2013; Venema, 2016).

Current research does not appear to pinpoint how these ideologies manifest during interviews because there are very few critical discourse studies that highlight them. This study endeavours to fill that gap by asking:

(1) What power relations and ideologies manifest in the dialogue between the RCMP officer and the indigenous child complainant during the interview?
(2) Do the findings suggest evidence of discursive Yentling by the RCMP officer? If so, how?

To answer these questions, the present study is informed by principles of critical discourse studies (CDS), ideology, and feminist approaches to critical discourse analysis.

Theory and methods

Inspired by Heydon's (2005) approach to investigate how power relations and ideologies manifest in the discursive negotiations of institutional representatives, the analysis of the police interview with the indigenous child is theoretically informed by CDS, ideology, and feminist approaches to CDS (FCDS). Furthermore, the concept of discursive Yentling is explored through combined lenses of FCDS (i.e. Lazar, 2018) and Brownmiller's (1975) assertion that rape should be defined as a violent act.

CDS and ideology

Rooted in *critical linguistics* research of the 1970s and 80's (Machin & Mayr, 2012), perhaps most directly with *Language and Control* (Kress et al., 1979) and *Language as Ideology* (Hodge & Kress, 1979), and *Language and Power* (Fairclough, 1989), critical discourse analysis (CDA) played a key role incentivizing linguistic scholars to rigorously investigate language in society. CDA, pluralistically termed CDS to reflect its various approaches and scholarly perceptions (Wodak & Meyer, 2016), not only reveals the *order of discourse* (i.e. Fairclough, 1989), but 'correspondingly emphasises ideology rather than just persuasion and manipulation' (Flowerdew & Richardson 2018, p. 15). Since CDS recognizes discourse as a vehicle for power, it also inspires political intervention and social change (Machin & Mayr, 2012; Wodak & Meyer, 2016). In the contexts of the present study, *ideology* manifests in the discursive negotiations of institutional representatives (e.g. police interviews) (Van Dijk, 2011) and acts as an interpretive frame that *ferments* historically rooted products/ideas of ruling classes, so that they become accepted, universal 'truisms' (Van Dijk, 2011).

Discursive Yentling and feminist CDS

The concept/term *Yentling* first appeared in medical literature referring to *Yentl syndrome* (Healy, 1991), where ischaemic heart disease in women was misdiagnosed because of predominantly male-related medical data informing diagnostic decisions (Merz, 2011). We adopt the term as a discursive illustration where, in the police interview, the male RCMP officer (syllogistically) *diagnoses* the female complainant about an act of sexualized violence from a male perspective. Discursive Yentling is informed by Lazar's (2018) *victim blaming* and *perpetrator mitigation*, and Brownmiller's (1975) assertion that rape is a violent act, divorced from sexuality, driven by male domination and female exploitation (MacLeod, 2010).

Androcentric assumptions of rape

In a critical study of a sexual assault case at a Canadian university, involving a male defendant and two female complainants, Ehrlich (2001) found undercurrents of androcentric assumptions in all forms of discourses throughout the legal processes (Lazar, 2018). Androcentric assumptions reproduce narratives of gender inequalities, in this case discursively manifested in blame for *not doing enough* to prevent rape, thereby implying consent because there did not seem to be sufficient resistance to the sexual *advances* of the male perpetrator, while simultaneously diminishing his culpability for the crime (Lazar 2018).

Victim blaming

For Lazar (2018), Ehrlich (2001) proves that androcentric assumptions about rape can lead to victim blaming. Drawing attention to a few points that resonate with victim blaming, Lazar (2018) argues that modals of obligation in a relational process, such as *'you should/shouldn't have ... '* suggests a measure of responsibility on the woman as the *actor* who brings the assault upon herself. Additionally, *victim responsibility* in a dialogue such as a police interview, can be illuminated by looking at transitivity and verb processes (i.e. Machin & Mayr, 2012; Teo, 2000). Lazar (2018) argues that transitivity structures not only purge alleged perpetrators of responsibility (e.g.: *he could not resist you*) but can position the woman as the *Actor* (e.g.: *you did not do something*), so that victim blaming is achieved by noting *her inability to do something about it*.

Perpetrator mitigation

Lazar (2018) illustrates three important points that achieve perpetrator mitigation. First, adjudication language can discursively re-construct 'rape' as 'a tragedy' or 'the event' or even a 'lapse in judgement,' and so on. This process of re-lexicalization can occur with other grammatical functions, such as transitivity structures, so that perpetrator accountability is lessened (Lazar, 2018). Second, '... blame sharing can mitigate culpability' (Lazar, 2018, p. 382); the defendant and the female victim are 'presented as responsible for the violence committed against the victim' (p. 382). Third, androcentric cultural stereotypes, such as (a) being in a drunken state and/or (b) unable to control male impulses, occasionally diminish perpetrator culpability because they are portrayed as victims themselves.

Brownmiller's foundation

Considered the 'cornerstone of feminist scholarship on rape' (MacLeod, 2010, p. 16), Brownmiller's (1975) arguments underscore the definition of rape as a violent, social problem. For Brownmiller (1975), violence against women is woven into patriarchal cultures to perpetuate male domination and female exploitation. In the context of the present study, when a police officer sexualizes rape, especially from male perspectivization, a facet of discursive Yentling is formed because it violates Brownmiller's (1975) foundation that rape is not a sexual act.

The present study argues that evidence of discursive Yentling aligns with androcentric assumptions about rape (Ehrlich, 2001), victim blaming, perpetrator mitigation (Lazar, 2018), the sexualization of rape (Brownmiller, 1975), and a general *misdiagnosis* from male perspectivizations (Healy, 1991) that any assault occurred.

Analysis

The data for the present study is a transcription of a police video, retrieved from Castanet.net (https://www.castanet.net/news/Kelowna/256862/Cop-makes-teen-relive-rape), initially obtained by Alanna Kelly (May 22, 2019), a reporter for Kelowna, B.C.'s Castanet News Service. The video features a child victim reporting her own sexual assault to the RCMP. Only twenty-six minutes was transcribed and analyzed because it represents the bulk of time when the RCMP officer and the child (the only participants) are completely alone.

We use Wodak and Meyer's (2016) Discourse Historical Approach (DHA), augmented with Machin and Mayr's (2012) observations of *Transitivity and Verb Processes* because it is a strong indicator for ideologies, not only highlighting *who does what to whom*, etc., but what things are absent from the action (Machin & Meyer, 2012), such as perpetrator responsibility (Lazar, 2018). The DHA (Wodak & Mayr, 2016) underpins how persons, objects, phenomena/events, and processes are linguistically referenced; what characteristics, qualities and features are attributed to them; what arguments are employed; what attitudes and stances are expressed; does illocutionary force intensify or mitigate expression. By including Machin and Mayr's (2012) transitivity and verb processes, we pay attention to material, mental, behavioural, verbal, relational, and existential processes. Evidence of discursive Yentling is drawn from the combined findings that resonate with androcentric assumptions about rape (Ehrlich, 2001), victim blaming and/or perpetrator mitigation (i.e. Lazar, 2018), and if the alleged assault is nominalized, predicated, framed, or argued to be a sexualized act (i.e. Brownmiller, 1975).

The following sections present specific findings immediately followed by brief discussions that show their salience in the present study. By bringing them together, readers less familiar with some of the analytical steps (forthcoming) may gain easier access to the inferences and assertions drawn from the data.

Discourse historical approach

Nomination strategies

There are few synecdoche's, membership devices, or proper nouns in the interview. However, there are generalized, professional, and relation anthroponyms such as 'the police' or 'you people,' noted by the Child (hereafter, Child will be represented in the uppercase), or in 'Doctor,' 'someone,' 'people,' 'nobody,' 'mystery-person,' 'person' or 'your step-father.' There are numerous deictics (I, you we, they) but nothing too specific that speaks of anyone in any abundance, other than the Child.

The discursive constructions of the objects/phenomena/events in the interview include the following:

- Concrete – *clothes; hospital; jail; morning-after pill; house; drugs; bite-mark.*
- Abstract – *point; consent; lie; trouble; justice; stuff; crime; time; questions; investigative costs; things; advantage; history; inclination; evidence; examination; inclination; reason; reaction; allegation; assault; closure; choice; imagination; concerns; misunderstanding; freedom; it; yesterday, dishonest, advances.*

Concrete and abstract discursive constructions, by contrast, can give specific reference or obscure via vagueness (Wodak & Meyer, 2016). Much like placing pieces on a workshop table, these categories aid the analyst in gaining a 'bird's eye view' to begin mapping patterns in social interaction and the discursive strategies manifesting around them. In the concrete and abstract constructions listed above, we begin to see that the topics on which the RCMP officer concentrates are noticeably peripheral to the alleged assault.

Machin and Mayr (2012) remind us that *material* processes require an actor and a goal, and help us reveal the beneficiary of that distinction, but *mental* processes are more complicated, divided into three sub-categories (perception; affection; cognition) and yield insight into feelings or states of mind. *Behavioural* processes, semantically close to other processes, can identify the experience of a single participant, while *verbal* processes reveal agency in the 'sayer', the 'receiver,' and the particular verb used (Machin & Mayr, 2012). *Relational* verbs are states of being that can camouflage opinion to make it appear as fact (e.g. people *have* worries about …), much like *existential* processes, often manifested from 'be' verbs, that can obscure agency (e.g. There has been an assault) (Machin & Mayr, 2012). The processes discovered in the interview include the following:

- Material – *attack; taking; picked up; kissing; pushed; get; did; raped; stopped; abused; found; open; close; examined; set; drugged; dropped; confront; threaten;*
- Mental – *thinking; thought; know; scared; want; interpret; knew; looks; understand; believes; remember; wonder; doubt; appreciate*
- Behavioural – *going; lying; lie; resist; believe; assumed; meant; ignore; tries; checked; compare; avoid; concerned; allowed; need; hesitate; investing; exaggerated; walking*
- Verbal – *say; tell; said; told; expressed; explain; telling; alleged*
- Relational – *have; has; were*
- Existential – *happened; hurting; being; hurt*

After looking at how the persons, objects, phenomena/events, and processes are discursively constructed in the interview (nomination) (Wodak & Meyer, 2016), we find certain measures of overlexicalization (i.e. Machin & Mayr, 2012) and re-lexicalization (Lazar, 2018) suggestive of the ideological predispositions of the RCMP officer. In this way, the RCMP officer diminishes the criminality of the alleged assault. Throughout the interview, the officer refers to the assault as *'it'* and *'something'* (that happened); details are nominated as *'stuff,' 'things,' 'lie/lies,' 'story,'* and *'allegation.'* This suggests a reluctance to attribute validity to the Child's account and corroborated by high instances of behavioural processes, such as *'lying/lie,' 'resist,' 'meant,' 'hesitate,'* and *'exaggerate.'* These behavioural processes are connected to a single actor, the Child, whose transitive behaviour is discursively constructed by the RCMP officer as unreliable. By projecting unreliability in these constructions, the RCMP officer is placing some measure of blame on the Child. These constructions are further corroborated in the forthcoming transitivity analysis.

Predication strategies

As noted by MacLeod (2010), agency is heavily one-sided, in favour of (in this case) the RCMP officer, who judges the discursive qualification of the Child's report. Table 1 lists a number of these instances in the interview alongside their devices. The discussion section will further illustrate their significance *in situ*.

Table 1 features several utterances that the analysis has identified as devices for predications strategies (i.e. Wodak & Meyer, 2016), such as metaphors (e.g. *dark room)*, implicatures (e.g. *turned on)*, and explicit predication (e.g. *you went along with it)*.

These predication characteristics (see Table 1) show that the officer positions the Child as unable to know what 'scared' means, mitigating the legitimacy of an alleged assault by confusing *'rape'* with *'taken advantage of'* or giving plausible consent by suggesting she *'just went along with it,'* and *'didn't say no,'* or suggesting gratification by asking if she was *'turned on'* and if it compared to other *'sexual experiences,'* or suggesting a profit from dishonesty; that she just *'went along with it'* because she *'needed the pill,'* or that her *'hesitation,'* interpreted by the officer as an inability to *'run screaming from the house like you see*

Table 1. Predication Strategies by the RCMP officer.

Time	Utterance(s)	Devices
00:27	Child: ... I was just scared ... RCMP: scared of what? If I walk into a dark room, I'm not *just* scared. I 'm scared that maybe there 's someone hiding in the dark -	Metaphor; disqualifying the Child's claim because she cannot specify an abstraction
01:48	you were 'raped' or 'taken advantage of'?	Comparison; Presupposition; Implicature
02:42	So, you just went along with it?	Explicit predication of the Child's plausible consent
03:24	CHILD: I have a friend ... two nights ago he tried this with her, but she said 'No!' RCMP: Since she said 'no,' he stopped ... since you didn't, he didn't stop. Right?	Comparison; alluding the Child's experience was due to her inaction
07:20	were you at all turned on during this ... at all?	Evocation of sexual enjoyment
07:43	CHILD: Yeah ... it hurt a lot RCMP: ... it hurt a lot? at the beginning?	Implicature; interrogative prepositional phrase
07:48	OK ... how does that compare to experiences you 've had in the past, sexually?	Alluding; sexualizing the assault
08:07	did the doctor give you any inclination about what happened?	Presupposition; doctor is qualified to determine the truth of 'what happened'
08:56	you came up with this ... because you were scared you might be pregnant ... you needed to get 'the pill'	Alluding/implicature; the Child is profiting from dishonesty
11:49	CHILD: I didn't necessarily say no but I didn't consent to it like I said no a couple times RCMP: but you went along with it	Explicit predication (second example)
12:31	if you were being one hundred percent truthful with me, this would have been a lot smoother.	Negative evaluative attribute / relational process
15:09	instead of running away screaming out of the house like you see on movies, you hesitated	Comparison; disqualifying the child's actions as 'inaction'

in the movies,' results in her misfortune. Collectively, these predications disqualify the Child's assertion that she was sexually assaulted because they create a narrative of false motives and misbehaviour.

Argumentation and perspectivization strategies

Findings of the RCMP officer's argumentation (justification and questioning of claims) and perspectivization (positioning of one's point of view) have been combined in Table 2.

Table 2 identifies several utterances as devices for argumentation and perspectivization (Wodak & Meyer, 2016), such as challenging the Child's perception of the alleged assault (e.g. *scared or what?*) or arguing against the child's claim that she was in pain (e.g. *It hurt a lot? At the beginning?*). The RCMP officer's arguments and perspectivizations challenge the Child's claims (see Table 2). He asks, 'what are you scared of?' as if to question the normative righteousness that assaults can be 'scary,' then threatens her with 'you say you've been raped so people have to go to jail,' as if to contend her actions will result in the incarceration of a (neutrally constructed) 'person.'

The officer further challenges the allegation of assault by persistently inserting tag questions throughout the interview:

CHILD: ... it hurt a lot.

RCMP: It hurt a lot? ... at the beginning?

These challenge and invalidate the Child's claim of truth/assertions by suggesting she is not certain or correctly recalls 'what happened' or that the assault could have just been *rough sex* or *misunderstood advances*. By arguing with the Child's claims that she was in pain, the RCMP officer continues to project a sexualized narrative by presupposing the pain lessens over time.

Intensification/mitigation strategies

By modifying the illocutionary force of his assertions, the RCMP officer mitigates or intensifies his or comments during the interviews. Those utterances are illustrated in Table 3.

Table 2. Argumentation and perspectivization.

Time	Utterance(s)	Devices
0:20	CHILD: I was scared ... RCMP: scared of what?	Metaphor; perspectivization of skepticism about the Child's claim
00:27	Yeah, what are you scared of?	Questioning the normative righteousness that the assault was scary
03:45	what do you 03:45 mean by 'justice'?	Questioning the Child's desire for justice
05:16	when you say you think you 've been drugged and 'I 've been raped,' people need to go to jail.	Challenging the Child's claim; Referential nominalisation of 'people'
07:18	RCMP: were you at all turned on during this, at all?	Challenging the Child's claim of assault by suggesting enjoyment
07:45	CHILD: ... it hurt a lot. RCMP: It hurt a lot? ... at the beginning?	Challenging the Child's claim, as above
11:08	RCMP: it seems to me ... it is not even what happened	Challenging the Child's normative righteousness; positioning skepticism
18:03	what would you have to gain by not telling the truth about something like this?	Challenging the Child to justify her actions

In Table 3, the RCMP officer's illocutionary force did not intensify. However, he engaged in a persistent tone of calm mitigation while listening and responding to the child's recollection of the alleged assault (e.g. *sorts of things*), most notably in the numerous pauses/silences. The RCMP officer mitigates more than intensifies the illocutionary force of his expressions (see Table 3) by engaging in a persistent, epistemic stance of skepticism, evident in challenges for the Child to define '*scared,*' '*justice,*' and '*sexual experience.*' He invokes a desire to '*put closure to this,*' as if the interview will conclude the matter, underscored by '*do you think you've been helped?*' as if to suggest the matter is ready to be put to rest. Perhaps most notably, mitigation is evident in the numerous and lengthy hesitations by the officer. There are thirteen silent pauses between questions, each lasting more than five seconds, suggesting the RCMP officer's reluctance to acquiesce to the Child's allegations of rape and presenting a notable distancing from that possibility.

Transitivity

By highlighting *what* is being done, by *whom, when, where* and *how,* transitivity plays a key role in understanding meaning-making (Machin & Mayr, 2012). In the context of the present study, the RCMP officer *projects* the Child as the 'doer' or 'actor' in several processes.

In Table 4, the child is 'doing' many things that places much agency on her as an active, yet dishonest, participant in the alleged assault (e.g. *telling a story; didn't resist; alleging*).

The transitivity analysis largely features the Child as the main actor in much of the interview, projected by the RCMP officer's dialogue. He presents the Child as someone whose misfortune is due to her inability to *run away, fight back, resist, say 'no,' or react timely (hesitate)*. For these reasons, the officer's transitive structures illustrate the Child as *telling a story, making false allegations, lying, being dishonest, not 100% truthful, telling things that are not consistent* because he feels she just *went along with it*, or was *turned on* by the experience. These ideological positionings resonate with the other findings to challenge the validity the Child's claims and diminish the criminality of the alleged assault.

Yentling

Discursive Yentling is a theoretical amalgam of victim blaming, perpetrator mitigation, and sexualized violence against women/girls from an androcentric perspective of rape

Table 3. Intensification/mitigation.

Time	Utterance(s)	Devices
01:18, 02:29, 04:11, 04:45, 06:16, 08:17, 13:05, 17:38, 18:08, 18:44, 19:31, 21:08, 22:14, 22:35, 23:51	mm-hmm … / yeah … / mmm-k …	Forms of hesitation; silent pauses lasting more than 5 s
03:45	What do you mean by justice?	Mitigation; indirect diminishment of the potential assault
04:03	What kind of help do you need?	Mitigation; indirect; help requires an explanation
05:17	You say you think you 've been drugged …	Mitigation; Child is the actor in the verbal process
12:54	You remember all sorts of things …	Mitigation; vague expression in the referential construction
13:37	We at least need to … put some closure to this …	Mitigation; Obligatory modality

Table 4. Child Transitivity from the perspective of the RCMP.

Time	Utterance(s)
00:13	didn't resist him (the perpetrator)
00:44 / 03:35	didn't say no
02:42 / 11:49	just went along with it
04:23	telling a story
04:35	didn't fight back
05:08	hopeful the person would go to jail
06:19	concerned about pregnancy
06:30	wanted free birth-control pills
06:58	didn't do anything to get away
07:18	Turned on (by the assault)
07:21	(sexually) responsive (to the assault)
11:58	not allowed to lie
12:06	telling things that are inconsistent
12:16	made an allegation
12:31	not being 100% truthful
12:45	remembers all sorts of 'things'
13:25	understand the cost of investigation
15:13	hesitated (during assault)
15:53	alleging rape
18:37	gain by not telling the truth
19:01	Over-exaggerating (the assault)
21:16	Regret telling (reporting the assault)
22:36	Were into it (the assault)

(Brownmiller, 1975; Ehrlich, 2001; Lazar, 2018). As revealed by the DHA (Wodak & Meyer, 2016) and the transitivity analysis (Machin & Mayr, 2012), the following excerpts are categorized in Table 5.

Table 5 amalgamates devices of victim blaming (e.g. *you were responsive*), perpetrator mitigation (e.g. *his advances*), and sexualized violence (e.g. *were you turned on … ?*). This discussion brings all the sampled utterances, featured in Tables 1–4, together to show how discursive Yentling manifests during the interview.

This study initially asked *what power relations and ideologies manifested in the dialogue between the RCMP officer and the indigenous child complainant during the interview?* The findings reveal the officer exerts his authority over the situation by dominating the direction of the dialogue. Instead of listening, he offers connotative undercurrents by discursively constructing unreliability in her behaviour, predicating her actions as untrustworthy or questionable, insinuating she may have enjoyed the encounter, invalidating her assertions, and mitigating anything she claims by responding with thirteen instances of lengthy silence.

This study additionally asked: *do the findings suggest evidence of discursive Yentling by the RCMP officer?* As per Lazar (2018) (see Table 5), victim blaming occurs throughout the interview, notably when the officer warns the Child that *'people need to go to jail'* – the obligatory modal infers a threat that a neutrally constructed *'person'* could be incarcerated because of the Child's actions – this is repeated three times during the interview. Transitive structures (see Table 4) also blame the Child for not *resisting, running away,* or *saying no* or that she is *lying, not telling the truth, making up stories,* or *being 100% truthful*. As for perpetrator mitigation, the officer insists on clarifying why the Child is 'scared' (three times) or if she misunderstood the man's 'advances' – disqualifying the victim while positively constructing the perpetrator – or noting a *silver lining* to the assault that *'he used a condom'* when she was *'taken advantage of,'* the latter suggesting a diminutive, criminal

Table 5. Evidence of Discursive Yentling by the RCMP Officer.

Time	Utterance	Yentling Form/Significance
00:27; 00:34; 00:37	what are you scared of?	Perpetrator mitigation / suggests the 'event' (assault) is not scary
01:48	Taken advantage of ...	Perpetrator mitigation /'taken advantage of' is contrasted against 'rape'
01:57	You were sexually raped?	Sexualizing rape / explicit reference
05:19	people need to go to jail ... there 's no other way around that, right?	Victim blaming / 'people' are neutral; obligatory modal 'need' implies child responsibility
06:16	you concerned you might have gotten pregnant?	Victim blaming / the child is the actor to whom pregnancy is a concern and a reason to report assault
06:44	RCMP: he wore a condom, right? CHILD: ... yeah, he did. RCMP: Do you remember what colour it was? CHILD: no. RCMP: do you remember him putting it on? CHILD: yeah. RCMP: yeah? How long did it take him ... ? CHILD: five seconds.	- Sexualizing rape / forcing the child to relive the experience as a sexual act - Perpetrator mitigation / 'he wore a condom' implies he was acting conscientiously.
07:20	RCMP: ... were you at all turned on during this ... at all?	Sexualizing rape / it was possibly enjoyable
07:25	you weren't at all responsive to his advances?	- Sexualizing rape / suggesting the possibility of 'behavioural' or implied consent - Perpetrator mitigation; the abstract nomination of 'advances' is a positive construction
07:48	how does that compare to experiences you 've had in the past, sexually?	Sexualizing rape; comparison of rape with a sexual experience
08:34	just to kind of give you some relief ... a condom is a pretty good way to avoid getting a sexually transmitted disease ... just so you are not losing sleep over that ...	Sexualizing rape; perpetrator mitigation; implying the assault is less worrisome because a condom was used
08:51	part of the reason you came up with this	Victim blaming; predication in the behavioural process 'came up' disqualifies the truthfulness of the Child
09:37 / 12:51	you remember a lot of things / all sorts of things	Victim blaming / 'things' are disqualified as unconfirmed abstractions rather than details of an assault
13:28	this costs a lot of money	Victim blaming / the Child's report is costing the RCMP and taxpayer's money
22:46	you think he legitimately honestly thought that you were into it?	Perpetrator Mitigation / distancing the perpetrator from responsibility; challenging the Child's certainty

offence. As per Brownmiller (1975), the RCMP officer sexualizes the alleged rape by suggesting the Child might have been *turned on*, or that it could be comparable to *sexual experience*, or that consent may have been implied because she was *responsive*. For these reasons, there is sufficient support and evidence of discursive Yentling on the part of the RCMP officer because he blames the Child, diminishes the criminal intent of the alleged perpetrator, and sexualizes a violent act.

Conclusion

Inspired by a Canadian crisis in high instances of sexual assault on women and a lack of critical discourse studies in those legal contexts, the present study illuminated a culture of ideologically rooted skepticism in police services towards victims of sexual violence.

Analyses of the interview transcripts found that power relations and ideologies favour the RCMP officer, who dominates the dialogue with accusations of misbehaviour, narratives of disbelief, and an overall atmosphere of skepticism. Discursive Yentling is evident in victim blaming, perpetrator mitigation, and the sexualization of rape. Future investigations could focus on discursive Yentling in other legal forums where institutional authority challenges female complainants of sexual assault. The findings also suggest a need to study the plight of Canadian Indigenous Canadian women and girls (Conroy & Cotter, 2017) in similar circumstances. The implications of this study hopefully provoke more considered police interview techniques for potential victims of sexual assault and inculcate a culture of fresh understanding in Canadian law enforcement. According to Castanet.net, the RCMP officer was demoted, removed from his position, but maintains employment with the RCMP at another location. Prejudicial perspectivization by officers *in situ* should not override the voices of alleged victims of rape, who, despite intense suffering and the certainty of humiliation and publicized scrutiny, have chosen to step forward because they seek help and justice.

Disclosure statement

No potential conflict of interest was reported by the author(s).

References

Atkinson, J. M., & Drew, P. (1979). *Order in court*. Springer.
Brownmiller, S. (1975). *Against our will: Men, women, and rape*. Simon & Schuster.
Canadian Association of Chiefs of Police (CAPC). (2019, November 7). Canadian Framework for Collaborative Police Response on Sexual Violence. Retrieved January 5, 2022, from http://cacp.ca/
Chen, Y., & Ullman, S. E. (2010). Women's reporting of sexual and physical assaults to police in the national violence against women survey. *Violence Against Women*, *16*(3), 262–279. https://doi.org/10.1177/1077801209360861
Conroy, S., & Cotter, A. (2017). *Self-reported sexual assault in Canada, 2014*. Juristat: Canadian centre for justice statistics. Ministry of Justice, Canada.
Ehrlich, S. L. (2001). *Representing rape: Language and sexual consent*. Psychology Press.
Fairclough, N. (1989). *Language and power*. Longman.
Flowerdew, J., & Richardson, J. E. (2018). *The Routledge handbook of critical discourse studies*. Routledge.
Greeson, M. R., Campbell, R., & Fehler-Cabral, G. (2014). Cold or caring? Adolescent sexual assault victims' perceptions of their interactions with the police. *Violence and Victims*, *29*(4), 636–651. https://doi.org/10.1891/0886-6708.VV-D-13-00039
Haworth, K. (2017). The discursive construction of evidence in police interviews: Case study of a rape suspect. *Applied Linguistics*, *38*(2), 194–214. https://doi.org/10.1093/applin/amv009
Healy, B. (1991). The Yentl syndrome. *New England Journal of Medicine*, *325*(4), 274–276. https://doi.org/10.1056/NEJM199107253250408

Heydon, G. (2005). *The language of police interviewing*. Palgrave Macmillan.
Hodge, R., & Kress, G. R. (1979). *Language as ideology*. Routledge.
Kress, G., Fowler, R., Hodge, B., & Trew, T. (1979). *Language and control*. Routledge.
Lazar, M. M. (2018). Feminist critical discourse analysis. In J. Flowerdew & J. E. Richardson (Eds.), *The Routledge handbook of critical discourse studies* (pp. 372–387). Routledge.
Machin, D., & Mayr, A. (2012). *How to do critical discourse analysis: A multimodal introduction*. Sage.
MacLeod, N. J. (2010). Police interviews with women reporting rape: A critical discourse analysis [Doctoral dissertation]. Aston University. https://doi.org/10.48780/publications.aston.ac.uk.00015206
McMillan, L., & Thomas, M. (2009). Police interviews of rape victims: Tensions and contradictions. In M. Horvath and J. Brown (Eds.), *Rape: Challenging Contemporary Thinking* (pp. 255–280). Devon: Willan Publishing. https://doi.org/10.4324/9781843927129-23
Merz, C. N. B. (2011). The Yentl syndrome is alive and well. *European Heart Journal*, *32*(11), 1313–1315. https://doi.org/10.1093/eurheartj/ehr083
Palmater, P. (2016). Shining light on the dark places: Addressing police racism and sexualized violence against indigenous women and girls in the national inquiry. *Canadian Journal of Women and the Law*, *28*(2), 253–284. https://doi.org/10.3138/cjwl.28.2.253
Powell, M. B., & Cauchi, R. (2013). Victims' perceptions of a new model of sexual assault investigation adopted by Victoria police. *Police Practice and Research*, *14*(3), 228–241. https://doi.org/10.1080/15614263.2011.641376
Razack, S. H. (2016). Sexualized violence and colonialism: Reflections on the inquiry into missing and murdered indigenous women. *Canadian Journal of Women and the Law*, *28*(2), i–iv. https://doi.org/10.3138/cjwl.28.2.285
Rich, K., & Seffrin, P. (2012). Police interviews of sexual assault reporters: Do attitudes matter? *Violence and Victims*, *27*(2), 263–279. https://doi.org/10.1891/0886-6708.27.2.263
Starzynski, L. L., Ullman, S. E., Townsend, S. M., Long, L. M., & Long, S. M. (2007). What factors predict women's disclosure of sexual assault to mental health professionals? *Journal of Community Psychology*, *35*(5), 619–638. https://doi.org/10.1002/jcop.20168
Teo, P. (2000). Racism in the news: A critical discourse analysis of news reporting in two Australian newspapers. *Discourse & Society*, *11*(1), 7–48. https://doi.org/10.1177/0957926500011001002
Van Dijk, T. A. (2011). *Discourse studies: A multidisciplinary approach*. Sage.
Venema, R. (2019). Making judgments: How blame mediates the influence of rape myth acceptance in police response to sexual assault. *Journal of Interpersonal Violence*, *34*(13), 2697–2722. https://doi.org/10.1177/0886260516662437
Venema, R. M. (2016). Police officer schema of sexual assault reports: Real rape, ambiguous cases, and false reports. *Journal of Interpersonal Violence*, *31*(5), 872–899. https://doi.org/10.1177/0886260514556765
Wodak, R., & Meyer, M. (2016). *Methods of critical discourse studies*. Sage.

'If she asked for settlement money, she must not be a real victim': An interdisciplinary analysis of the discourse of victims and perpetrators of sexual violence

Huijae Yu

ABSTRACT
This paper analyses the discourse surrounding a high-profile sexual assault case in South Korea. While most research on language and sexual violence has focused on the media portrayal or online resistance movement, not much has focused on the language and the law. Using Critical Discourse Analysis and rhetoric, this present paper seeks to show the importance of value of paying closer attention to legal decision-making process, showing how this can make a significant contribution to the literature. The analysis reveals two distinctive discourses at work. One is that victims must embody and display certain characteristics as a 'pure and destroyed' individual in order to avoid being dismissed or appearing untrustworthy. The second is that the perpetrators represent themselves as victims seeking to makes it the goal of the court to protect the perpetrators' rights, rather than those of the victims.

Introduction

Sexual violence trials have long been criticized as a site where gender discrimination is highly visible. Researchers from a range of academic fields show that rape myths (Burt & Estep, 1981), such as portraying victims of sexual violence as passive, naïve, and innocent, have damaging consequences both for the victims who fall into this stereotype and for those who do not (Clark, 1992; Cuklanz, 1996; Gill, 2011; Meyers, 1997; Wykes, 2001; Wykes & Welsh, 2009). These discourses of rape, which involve legitimate victims have far reaching consequence in the sentencing of individuals involved in sexual violence. Specifically in rape trials, a particularly constitutive role is ascribed to language since there is often no physical evidence, and thus cases often rest on the testimony of the relevant parties. As feminist discourse analysts have criticized, these rape trials are a site where gender inequalities have the most damaging consequences (e.g. Ehrlich, 2001), to the point of being described as 'rape of the second kind' (Matoesian, 2001, p. 676) or 'judicial rape' (Lees, 1996, p. 161).

Considering how a rather large body of research has shown widespread injustice and discrimination in rape trails in Western culture, Holoshitz and Cameron (2014) state that there has not been enough research about language and rape in non-Western cultures. Although there is a growing body of work on language and sexual violence in East

Asian countries, focusing on the specific cultures that support sexual violence (Dalton, 2019; Tsunoda, 2013; Wang, 2017), a political system or media portrayal (Hong, 2009; Kim, 2006b; Rose Luqiu & Liao, 2021; Yi, 2021; Yu, 2020), and the resistance movement against rape (Zeng, 2019), the relationship between language and law in regard to sexual violence remains largely unaccounted for.

In South Korea, even though a few studies have noted that the understanding of sexual violence itself has been constituted mainly around male experiences (Kim, 2015; Lee, 2018), there is an absence of research in the field of Korean linguistics and Discourse Analysis investigating the language of legal decision-making in actual cases. Part of the reason for this is simply the difficulty of obtaining the data. In South Korea, non-authorized people cannot record court proceedings under any circumstances, and official recordings or transcripts are never released for academic purpose except very few Supreme Court cases. Therefore, this study endeavours to take a step towards overcoming this problem by suggesting a methodology to enable an indirect discourse analysis of courtroom discourse. The objectives of this paper are as follows:

(1) To evaluate the texts' rhetorical effectiveness in regard to building logos, ethos, and pathos.
(2) To examine each text's logical soundness with the analysis of their argumentation structure.

Methodology

Rhetoric and enthymeme

Responding to a call for interdisciplinary research in the field of CDS, this paper combines rhetorical analysis with a methodology from CDS. Rhetoric, according to Aristotle, is the capacity to notice the available means of persuasion (Murphy et al., 2013). Therefore, incorporating rhetorical analysis into the discourse analysis can foster a detailed analysis of the speakers' strategies and what goals they intend to achieve via such means.

An important concept in Aristotle's rhetoric is a trifecta of persuasion techniques: logos, ethos, and pathos (Murphy et al., 2013). Logos refers to the logic of an argument that aims to prove or dispute a speaker's conclusion; ethos is related to the speaker's personal character; and pathos pertains to putting the audience into an emotional state in which the speaker's argument will be more easily accepted. Therefore, rhetorically effective speech not only needs sound logic but also needs to foster a good image of the speaker and to be able to move the audience's emotions.

Aristotle also introduced the concept of 'enthymeme' as a persuasive strategy (Murphy et al., 2013). Unlike a syllogism, which has two overt premises, an enthymeme typically has only one premise with one premise left unstated. One crucial difference is that the unstated premise in an enthymeme tends to be a matter of likelihood rather than absolute truth as represented in Table 1. This premise represents an assumption, a statement, a proposition or an ideal that the speaker presumes, and thus can be deduced in a reverse order with the conclusion and the stated premise. This unstated premise must have a reasonable level of probability and likelihood of being accepted, and the whole argument becomes more effective as this hidden premise becomes better accepted (Hill, 1972).

Table 1. Comparison between syllogism and enthymeme.

Syllogism	Enthymeme
(Premise 1) All men are mortal.	(Premise 1 - unstated) All men are strong.
(Premise 2) Socrates is a man.	(Premise 2) Plato is a man.
(Conclusion) Socrates is mortal.	(Conclusion) Plato is strong.

As Fairclough (2015) states, 'the fact that we can show fallacies in [one]'s argument does not mean that it will be widely perceived as fallacious, and we must consider what might make the argument ... persuasive' (p. 111). Given that many arguments in a judicial setting incorporate elements designed to make the speech not only logical but also more appealing, rhetoric provides a valuable set of tools for the present study in its examination of the persuasiveness.

Critical discourse studies and the structure of practical reasoning

While rhetoric concerns how effective and persuasive an argument is, one of the concerns in CDS is manipulation and ideology. Although this manipulation and ideology are sometimes quite apparent, at other times they can be naturalized in discourses. CDS, therefore, endeavours to denaturalize and unearth such manipulative and ideological elements within discourses.

One particularly useful framework for this analysis comes from Fairclough and Fairclough (2013), which itself was developed based on the works of Audi (2006) and Walton (2007). Fairclough and Fairclough (2013) suggest using a structure of practical reasoning to analyse political discourses with premises such as a goal, values, circumstances, an alternative action, and negative consequences, all in support of the conclusion that the agent (presumably) ought to do a certain action.

The problem with such structure is that it is simply not suitable for legal contexts. According to Aristotle's distinguishment of the three different branches of rhetoric (Murphy et al., 2013) – deliberative, judicial, and epideictic – the structure proposed by Fairclough and Fairclough (2013) is concerned with deliberative rhetoric, which has different characteristics from judicial rhetoric. This deliberate rhetoric deals with the future, while judicial rhetoric deals with the past. Deliberative rhetoric also deals with benefits and losses, while judicial rhetoric deals with justice (Murphy et al., 2013). Therefore, I suggest an amended structure for judicial reasoning as shown in Figure 1.

As with the original structure suggested by Fairclough and Fairclough (2013), this structure also focuses on the Claim for Action, as in 'Defendant should be found guilty' or 'Defendant should be found not guilty', supported by the Goal based on a certain Value. One way in which this proposed structure differs from the original structure is that the original structure suggests a circumstance premise about a general situation, while this structure has a more specified premise: a premise about the damage the speaker suffered. Another difference from Fairclough and Fairclough (2013) is that the argument contains an additional set of forensic arguments acting as premises for the Claim for Action. In the forensic argument, the focus is on whether the defendant committed the crime,[1] and the argument is further elaborated by various types of evidence. However, such evidence does not automatically lead to a conclusion. For instance, if someone asks for settlement money, it does not necessarily mean that the victim is

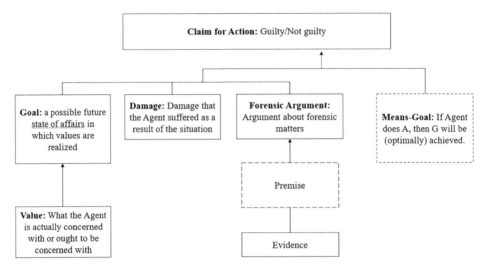

Figure 1. Structure of practical reasoning for judicial rhetoric (adapted from Fairclough & Fairclough, 2013).

lying, and that sexual assault did not happen. Such a conclusion requires another unstated premise (an assumption) as a bridge: 'If someone asks for settlement money, the person lying and is not sexually assaulted', which follows the structure of an enthymeme. With this more specified circumstance premise (as a Damage premise) and additional argument set, the suggested framework will be more adequate for analysing legal arguments. In this paper, I will be using this framework and analyze each text's argumentational structure into the diagram suggested in Figure 1.

Data

This analysis concerns a sexual violence case in South Korea, which I will briefly summarize here with contexts. The case is about an alleged sexual assault that occurred at a restaurant where a male customer touched another female customer's body. This case attracted a lot of attention when the perpetrator's wife posted her side of story on a website and later created a Blue House petition[2] arguing that her husband had been wrongly found guilty. This case focused on a piece of physical evidence: a CCTV video. Although the perpetrator was found guilty in the first trial, his wife claimed that the CCTV footage did not show her husband physically touching the victim's body, and that her husband had been wrongfully convicted. This petition soon became a site of gender dispute in Korea; some claimed that the husband did commit sexual assault, while others believed that the conviction represents a form of oppression against men. This case attracted much public attention and is still frequently quoted and referenced in public debates, online posts, or outdoor protests. It has become a symbol both for the need to address the issue of sexual violence and the backlash from those who feel that it is just another form of reverse discrimination against men.

The specific texts for the analysis come from written statements or interviews presented by the relevant victim and the perpetrator's side. The first text (Text A) comes from the petition circulated online by the perpetrator's wife,[3] which was posted after the first trial and before the second trial. The second text (Text B) is an interview with the victim of the same case around the same time.[4] Although these texts were presented outside of the courtroom and to the general public. The texts are both produced in the contexts of legal procedure, therefore bearing characteristics of language used in the judicial contexts. In the section below, I will present the argumentation structure of the texts and analyse their respective rhetorical effectiveness.

Argumentation structure and rhetorical analysis

Text A: perpetrator's post[5]

The speaker of this text is the perpetrator's wife, who argues that her husband did not commit a crime. A summary of the argumentation structure is portrayed in Figure 2.

As Figure 2 shows, Text A contains a Goal premise that *for [her] husband not to be abused by the law*. The Value premise is also hidden, but it can be inferred to be 'justice', which is a fundamentally good value. This Goal premise is coupled with the Damage premise: *[her husband] has been wronged* and *A family is utterly broken*. This premise is individual and specific to her situation (or someone whose family is accused of sexual assault) and might not appeal to much of the public. Nevertheless, the speaker's main Goal premise here specifies that her husband should not be *abused by the law*, suggesting that the current judicial system is corrupt and unfair, which affect most people in the society.

This text also presents an alternate future and the negative consequences of it as depicted in Figure 2. This potential future is based on her husband being found guilty of sexual assault during the first trial: *an innocent man [is] being marked as a criminal because of the law that discriminates against men*. This discourse of men being victims of reverse discrimination is a discourse commonly used as a backlash to the increasing

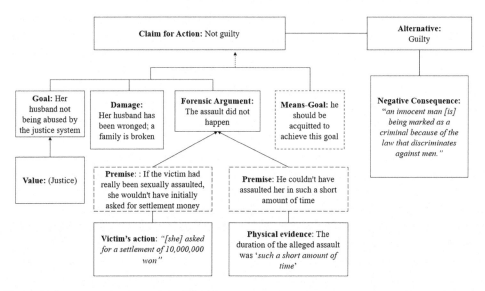

Figure 2. Argumentation structure of Text A.

feminist movements such as #MeToo movement. At the time in Korea, #MeToo movement and its backlash was gaining a lot of attention both in the media and among public, and the speaker precisely taps into this fear – that this will *break a family* and *ruin an innocent man's life*. This potential outcome is one of the most argued consequences by the feminism backlash movement (Yang, 2018), which means that it is accepted by many people believing in the backlash.

A large portion of Text A is devoted to the Forensic Argument that the sexual assault did not occur. Here, due to space considerations, I will present only the two main pieces of evidence suggested in this Forensic Argument premise: victim's actions and CCTV footage. The first piece of evidence pertains to the victim's actions. According to the wife's petition, the victim *asked for a settlement of 10,000,000 won*. The hidden premise here is 'if the victim had really been sexually assaulted, she would not have asked for settlement money', implying that the victim is lying to get money, damaging the ethos of the victim. This is also related to the discourse of portraying rape victims as innocent and naïve, which is widely accepted inside and outside of the courtroom, making this argument effective. Another piece of evidence is CCTV footage of the assault. The speaker emphasizes that the CCTV angle does not actually show his hands and that the duration of the alleged assault is *such a short amount of time*. This is coupled with the hidden premise of 'He could not have assaulted her in such a short amount of time', and leads to the conclusion that 'He did not grab her body'. Given that the CCTV footage was not decisive, this argument sounds logical, and therefore effectively establishes logos. This is possibly why this case, despite not involving anyone famous, gained a great deal of public attention, to the point of prompting people to gather in the streets as a protest against the #MeToo movement (Hangyere, 2018).

Text B: victim's interview

Text B is an interview with the victim, after this case received public attention. The structure of this text's argumentation is outlined below (Figure 3).

She states that her Goal is *the perpetrator admitting his wrongdoing and [her] receiving an apology*. As suggested in Figure 3, this is further supported by the Value premise: justice, which will be satisfied if the perpetrator *admits his wrongdoing*; truth, which *should not be twisted*; and respect, in that her body was violated and that this should not have happened. While these values (justice, truth, respect) are generally accepted as good values, especially in the context of sexual violence, the suggested goal is more individual and narrower than that of Text A, who argued for the justice in the whole judicial system.

This is partly due to the nature of this discourse; Text B is in direct response to Text A, focusing on establishing her ethos that Text A had damaged. It is not surprising that she chose to frame herself as an innocent victim wanting *only one thing: apology*, rather than pointing to wider issues of justice relating to gender discrimination in the judicial system. This means she is actively playing into the gendered discourse of innocent rape victims, which is further enhanced by the argument's Damage premise: *[her] day-to-day life is horrible due to all the cyber bullying [she is] receiving a lot of insults and hate*, she finds herself in *a truly terrifying and horrible situation*, *[her] life is ruined*, and *[she is] afraid to go out and feels like [her] life is in danger*. She also suggests an alternative imaginary in which the

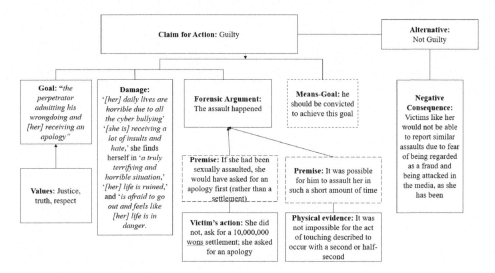

Figure 3. Argumentation structure of Text B.

perpetrator is acquitted and the resulting negative consequence that *a victim like [her] would not even be able to report the assault because of the fear that they might be framed as a fraud and be attacked by the media*. This is also an effective premise that invokes fear in public.

Much as in Text A, the main part of this text focuses on the Forensic Argument premise as shown in Figure 3. As a response to previous accusations, she rebuts the claim that her goal was to get money: *From the beginning, I claimed that there is no settlement without apology […] I have no idea why this ridiculous '10,000,000 won' story came out*. This is an effective argument that falsifies the previous claim while establishing her ethos as an innocent victim. Another refutation dealt with the CCTV footage. She argues that *it is in fact not impossible to touch like that within a second or even half a second*, referencing terms such as 'Eong-man-twi (grab ass and run)' and 'Seum-man-twi (grab boob and run)', both of which are newly coined words for a certain type of sexual assault. This also effectively rebuts the previous claim and establishes logos.

In sum, Text B devotes much of its discourse to logically rebutting the claims made in Text A. Although this effectively establishes logos and a certain amount of ethos, this is relatively weak compared to Text A's emotional expressiveness and strong evocation of fear. While the negative consequences suggested in Text B are truly terrifying, this consequence is limited to victims of sexual violence, a category to which relatively fewer people belong. On the other hand, the negative consequence as described in Text A suggests that the entire judicial system is against men and that people should rise up to prevent this. This is a highly persuasive claim, especially coming from the perpetrator's wife. Furthermore, in rebutting the previous claims, the victim had to emphasize that she was not a fraud and did not want the money in the first place, which in turn traps her in the frame established by Text A. Indeed, her speech gained relatively little attention compared to Text A, and many people continue to believe that the perpetrator was wronged, even though he was convicted in all later trials, including the final Supreme Court ruling.

Critical analysis

Nominal critique

Having presented the argumentation structures of the various texts and evaluated their effectiveness, now I turn to the matter of manipulation and ideology. First, a nominal critique of a text concerns itself with the criteria of acceptability, relevance, and sufficiency of the reasoning; it, therefore, asks such questions as 'Is this premise true (or acceptable)?' or 'Is this argument deductively valid (or inductively strong)?' (Audi, 2006). In addition, if the speaker himself did not believe in such premises and yet claimed to, this would be an instance of manipulation. However, this is not the case with the data presented here, since it is likely that all speakers truly believed in what they said. The problem arises not because the speaker did not believe in the premises but because premises themselves are flawed yet accepted as legitimate in the context of prevailing discourses. This does not mean that the arguers are not responsible for the manipulation. As Fairclough and Fairclough (2013) state, practical reasoning must include deliberating over other options for the goal, and a particular argument is always purposefully chosen to legitimate the claim and (mis)lead listeners to a particular conclusion. Following this, I will mainly examine whether the premises are acceptable, and the arguments are inductively strong, paying particular attention to the hidden premises in the Forensic Argument and Negative Consequences from the argumentation structure.

A common premises underlying the Forensic Arguments in Text A focus on the actions of the respective victims: 'If the victim really had been sexually assaulted, she would not have asked for settlement money first'. First, this premise was rebutted in Text B. The fact that the speaker of Text A abandoned her responsibility to confirm whether what she says is true means that she was manipulating her audience intentionally or not. Second, even if it were true, it is normal to ask for settlement money in any other type of crime, including physical assault. Hence, asking for settlement money in a sexual assault case should not be considered unusual. Therefore, the premise once again does not strongly support the conclusions.

Another noteworthy aspect of the perpetrator's discourses is their tendency to describe the negative consequences of the counterargument. Such negative consequences are explicitly stated in Text A when it describes a state in which *an innocent man [is] being marked as criminal because of the law that discriminates against men*. While not necessarily false, it is not inductively strong. According to recent statistics (Seoul Economics, 2015), there have been 148 cases in a given time period in which a female accuser was found guilty of false accusations, compared to a total number of 29,893 sexual violence convictions, making the likelihood of false accusation less than 0.5%. Again, although this premise was highly effective in provoking a sense of fear, it does not sufficiently support the claim.

Next, we turn our analysis to the victims' argumentation. In Text B, the victim suggests that she did not ask for 10,000,000 won but asked for a sincere apology first, with the implied premise that 'If she had been sexually assaulted, she would not have asked for the money'. This argument is not necessarily valid; as I stated in the previous section, it adapts and reproduces the same rape myth from the perpetrator's discourse. However, when compared to Text A's false claim ('she asked for a large sum of settlement money'), the truth value of this premise is True.[6] Another forensic argument from Text B is that the perpetrator was capable of touching her body within a short timeframe. Given that there are actual cases in which perpetrators grope victims very quickly (within a second) and run away, this argument is logically acceptable.

A negative consequence described in Text B is that subsequent victims will be afraid to report their victimization because of the fear that they might be regarded as frauds and be attacked by the media. In contrast to the perpetrator's fear of false conviction, this is statistically a more likely case. The percentage of women who report the sexual crimes they experience is only 12% (Ministry of Gender Equality and Family, 2010), and this figure is likely to be even lower since it only considers women who visited a consultation centre at least once. Thus, the argument in terms of negative consequences put forward in Text B is inductively strong.

Explanatory critique

Victimhood

Explanatory critique is concerned with the ideologies present in the discourses of a society as a whole. Because ideology can be naturalized within the discourse and language that we use, it might go unnoticed without detailed analysis. CDS, as such, aims to uncover this social wrong and unearth such naturalized ideology (Fairclough & Fairclough, 2013).

The most overt ideology in the perpetrator's discourse is that of 'ideal victimhood'. Texts A implies an ideal model of a rape victim: 'If the victim had been sexually assaulted, she would not have asked for settlement money'. This is problematic, not least because the implied connection is logically fallacious. As noted above, it is understandable for victims of sexual violence to return to their life or to ask for settlement money when doing so is deemed reasonable. Another problem is that judgements about criminality are applied to the actions of the victim, rather than those of the perpetrator. This conveniently locates the cause and reason for the assault in the victim, focuses on the victim's reactions rather than the perpetrator's assault, and moves accountability to the victim from the perpetrator. In other words, victims' failure to fit this stereotype produces a discursive construal that they are not the 'real' victim, and that the sexual violence must not have really occurred (Kim, 2006a; Lee, 2011; Ryu, 2018). Discourses such as Text A order victims of sexual violence to stay innocent and damaged, therefore not being able to ask for the rightful compensation. In other words, the premises pertaining to such victimhood claim for a perpetrator's innocence not only prevent a victim from being recognized as a victim but also from recovering and resuming their normal life afterwards.

Stealing victimhood

One notable finding of the analysis above is that victims and perpetrators use the exact same structure. This is particularly interesting given that this structure has a Damage premise. It is reasonable to assume that victims' discourse would include some type of statement about the damage they suffered because of the assault, but it might seem counterintuitive that perpetrators would do the same. However, most audiences would accept the perpetrators' 'Damage premises' as natural and logical parts of their argumentation. Furthermore, the basic argumentation structures used in Texts A and Texts B are nearly identical. Both pairs include Damage premises, Forensic Argument premises, and descriptions of the Negative Consequences of an alternative action. The structure of two discourses is nearly symmetrical. Provided that the structure has a Damage premise, it seems reasonable to infer that the structure is or should be typically used by victims. But, as seen above, the perpetrators adapt this structure to position themselves as 'the real victim'. This is strongly related to the ideology of victimhood, which dictates that the 'real' victims are those who are 'innocent and damaged'. Using this logic, the perpetrators argue that the real victims are not those who were assaulted, but those who have sustained the most damage, which they argue is they themselves.

Texts A exhibits the hallmarks of such an ideology. It effectively questions the victim's victimhood while accentuating the perpetrator's victimhood. The speaker questions the victim's victimhood and presents an image of the perpetrator's family that is now broken. It is worth noting that the Damage premises in the perpetrators' argument concern not the damage from the crime but rather the consequences of having committed a crime. Nevertheless, they present them as the damage they have suffered, emphasizing that they are the real victim of this situation. These discourses strip victimhood from victims to reinvent perpetrators as victims of 'the law that discriminates against men'. This ideology benefits already-privileged male perpetrators in the judicial system and take the little that was left for female victims: the position as a victim. In this discourse, the only visible agents are the 'wronged' perpetrators while the victims of sexual violence are nowhere to be seen.

Conclusion

This essay suggests a framework to enable the analysis of language and the law using the little discourse material available in South Korea. By adopting transdisciplinary research, this study evaluated the texts both in terms of their persuasiveness and effectiveness and in terms of manipulativeness and social justice. Following the analysis, the final section indicated how this discourse can put victims, who are already discriminated against, at an even greater disadvantage, both in terms of the judicial interpretation of cases and in terms of existing effects within a society.

Despite its results in showing how discourses in society show imbalanced opinions towards sexual violence, this paper is largely limited by its data. The two cases I presented, however representative they might be, is hardly a sufficient number to represent the whole, even the most of, society. Additionally, ideologies in a society are not made up by a single discourse genre; it is rather compromised by interaction between different texts and discourses. Therefore, future studies will benefit not only from adding more data, but also from adding data from various sources.

As a scholarly attempt to analyse the language involved in legal procedure in order to investigate problems concerning discrimination and gender, especially in South Korea, this paper showed that discourses surrounding sexual violence are hardly a place for a fair judgement. They are, in fact, a site where the interests and perspectives of the patriarchally privileged are amplified while those of female victims are diminished and even erased. With this understanding, I hope to have contributed to the unearthing of unfair ideologies and ushering of society to move to overcome such ideologies.

Notes

1. The criminal law regarding sexual assault in South Korea (mainly Criminal Act Article 298) have two main requisite elements: (1) whether a certain act (sexual assault) has happened (2) whether that act has been forced upon against the victim's will. I will be focusing on these two elements in the following analysis.
2. Blue House petitions are submitted through a government website where citizens can freely post their complaints. When a post gets enough petition from other people, a government official must answer to the post.
3. It is worth noting that all the speakers for the perpetrators are the perpetrators' female family members.
4. The first text was accessed through the online website it was posted, and the second one was retrieved from the media report who interviewed the victim. Both texts are open to public.
5. The text is actually from the perpetrator's wife but I will refer to the Text A as perpetrator's text for convience.
6. This evaluation is based on the sentencing from the first trial.

Disclosure statement

No potential conflict of interest was reported by the author(s).

References

Audi, R. (2006). *Practical reasoning and ethical decision*. Routledge.
Burt, M., & Estep, R. (1981). Who is a victim? Definitional problems in sexual victimisation. *Victimology*, *6*, 15–28.
Clark, K. (1992). The linguistics of blame: Representations of women in the sun's reporting of crimes of sexual violence. In M. Toolan (Ed.), *Language, text and context: Essays in stylistics* (pp. 208–224). Routledge.
Cuklanz, L. M. (1996). *Rape on trial*. University of Pennsylvania Press.
Dalton, E. (2019). A feminist critical discourse analysis of sexual harassment in the Japanese political and media worlds. In *Women's studies international forum* (p. 77). Pergamon.
Ehrlich, S. (2001). *Representing rape: Language and sexual consent*. Routledge.
Fairclough, I., & Fairclough, N. (2013). *Political discourse analysis: A method for advanced students*. Routledge.
Fairclough, N. (2015). A dialectical-relational approach to critical discourse analysis in social research. In: Meyer & Wodak (ed.), *Methods of critical discourse studies* (pp. 86–108). Sage.
Gill, R. (2011). Sexism reloaded, or, it's time to get angry again!. *Feminist Media Studies*, *11*(1), 61–71. https://doi.org/10.1080/14680777.2011.537029
Hangyere. (2018, October 28). Participants at the 'Gom-tang Restuarnat Sexual Assault' prorest "I came here after watching YouTube videos", Jang, S. & Lee, J. https://www.hani.co.kr/arti/society/women/867684.html
Hill, F. (1972). Conventional wisdom—traditional form—the president's message of November 3, 1969. *Quarterly Journal of Speech*, *58*(4), 373–386. https://doi.org/10.1080/00335637209383136
Holoshitz, T., & Cameron, D. (2014). The linguistic representation of sexual violence in conflict settings. *Gender and Language*, *8*(2), 169–184. https://doi.org/10.1558/genl.v8i2.169

Hong, J. (2009). The constitution of meaning of sexual violence - frame analysis of JoongAng daily newspaper and Hankyoreh. *Korean Journal of Broadcasting and Telecommunication Studies, 23*(5), 458–496.

Kim, D. (2006a). Reports about sexual violence and personal rights. 言論仲裁, *26*(2), 96–103.

Kim, H. (2006b). How to define a crime of rape: The meaning of consent. *Korean Criminological Review, 16*(4), 103–132.

Kim, M. (2015). The influence of perceived societal myth and self-devaluation on sexual violence victim's psychological health. *Korean Journal of Victimology, 23*(3), 173–200.

Lee, H. (2011). Critical review on elements of rape. *Yonsei Law Review, 21*(1), 33–66.

Lee, M. (2018). The gap between law and reality through the #Me Too movement. *Economy and Society, 120*, 12–35. https://doi.org/10.18207/criso.2018.120.12

Lees, S. (1996). *Carnal knowledge: Rape on trial*. Hamish Hamilton.

Matoesian, G. (2001). *Law and the language of identity: Discourse in the William Kennedy Smith rape trial*. Oxford University Press.

Meyers, M. (1997). *News coverage of violence against women*. Sage.

Ministry of Gender Equality and Family. (2010). 2010 *research on sexual violence cases*. https://www.korea.kr/archive/expDocView.do?docId=28859

Murphy, J. J., Katula, R. A., & Hoppmann, M. (2013). *A synoptic history of classical rhetoric*. Routledge.

Rose Luqiu, L., & Liao, S. X. (2021). Rethinking 'the personal is political:'Enacting agency in the narrative of sexual harassment experiences in China. *Discourse & Society, 32*(6), 708–727. https://doi.org/10.1177/09579265211023225

Ryu, H. (2018). An attempt at another interpretation for sexual intercourse by abuse of occupational authority. *WonKwang Journal of Law Research, 34*, 191–208. https://doi.org/10.22397/wlri.2018.34.2.191

Seoul Economics. (2015, March 26). For the money … for revenge … false accusation of rape skyrockets. Kim, H. https://www.hankookilbo.com/News/Read/201803261875692751

Tsunoda, Y. (2013). *Sei to hōritsu (sex and the law)*. Iwanami Shinsho.

Walton, D. (2007). *Media argumentation*. Cambridge University Press.

Wang, X. (2017). *Gender, dating and violence in urban China*. Routledge.

Wykes, M. (2001). *News, crime and culture*. Pluto Press.

Wykes, M., & Welsh, K. (2009). *Violence, gender and justice*. Sage.

Yang, W. (2018). "You can be a victim of wrongful conviction of sexual assault" #Youtoo movement debate, Hangook Ilbo.

Yi, J. (2021). Prioritizing free speech or the dignity of victims: Competing approaches to public discourse in Japan and South Korea. *Society, 58*(5), 380–383. https://doi.org/10.1007/s12115-021-00624-5

Yu, H. (2020). A social practice analysis on media reports about sexual violence. *Discourse & Cognition, 27*(2), 73–90. https://doi.org/10.15718/discog.2020.27.2.73

Zeng, J. (2019). You say# MeToo, I say# MiTu: China's online campaigns against sexual abuse. In B. Fileborn (Ed.), *# MeToo and the politics of social change* (pp. 71–83). Palgrave Macmillan.

Index

abortion 55–57, 59; complications 56, 57
Acharya, A. 53
androcentric assumptions 81, 82
Anghie, A. 34
antitrust 14, 20, 21, 23; discourse 14–24; jurisprudence 18, 23
argumentation 85, 98, 100; structure 92, 95, 98
Assimakopoulos, S. 9
Aston, S. 7
Atkinson, J. M. 79
AT&T-Time Warner merger 14–24
Audi, R. 93
Aydos, E. 7

Baldez, L. 54
BBC reporting 64–74
bicameral conference committee 54, 55, 57, 58
Bolivia 10, 27, 29–31
Bolivian constitution 28–29
Bolivian population 36
Brownmiller, S. 80–82, 88
Brownmiller's foundation 81–82

Cameron, D. 91
Canada 64, 67, 70, 71, 73, 74, 78–80; crisis 79
Cannie, H. 8–9
causalities 3, 6, 7, 65, 68
Chimni, B. S. 34
China 10, 64–66, 70, 72–74
colonial difference 32, 35, 36
communitarian state 28–32
competition 10, 14–16, 18–24; harming 19–20; law 14, 15; in media markets 17, 23; protecting 14–24
competitors 14–24; protecting 21–22
constitutional principles 28–30, 34, 36
constitutional validity 29, 30, 34
consumers 17, 20, 21, 23
Convention on the Elimination of All Forms of Discrimination against Women (CEDAW) 52–59
Cotterrell, R. 3

democracy 8, 9
depoliticization 64–74
digital platforms 20, 21
discourse analysis 7, 92
discourse historical approach (DHA) 82–86
discourses 5–7, 9, 10, 16, 18, 23, 32, 34, 54, 66, 68, 79, 80, 93, 95, 96, 99, 100; of victims 91–100
discursive script 8, 65, 66, 68, 69, 72, 74
discursive Yentling 78–82, 86–89
Dolhare, M. I. 28
double criminality test 71
Draude, A. 53
Drew, P. 79

education 55, 58
Ehrlich, S. L. 81
Englehart, N. A. 52
enthymeme 92, 94
environmental law 6, 7, 9
ethnicity 48
European constitutional discourses 27
explanatory critique 99
extraterritorial jurisdiction 65–74
extraterritorial laws 72

Fairclough, I. 93, 98
Fairclough, N. 5, 6, 68, 93, 98
Feminist Critical Discourse Analysis (FCDA) 52–59
Flowerdew, J. 9
forensic argument 93, 96, 97, 99, 100
Foucault, M. 3, 5, 6, 68
free trade 4, 6

gender 7, 54, 55, 57–59, 79, 100; inequalities 81, 91; relationality 53, 54
genealogy 41, 42, 49
global corporations 4, 9
Greeson, M. R. 79

Hall, M. A. 29
hate speech 7–9, 40, 43, 49
Heydon, G. 80

INDEX

Holoshitz, T. 91
Huawei 64, 66–72, 74

ideologies 2, 6, 10, 18, 79, 80, 82, 87, 93, 98–100
impact translation 53
incumbent competitors 21, 22
Indigenous peoples 29–36
individual rights 27, 32
interdisciplinary analysis 91
international treaties 30, 52, 54
intertextual genealogy 41, 42
intertextual micro-genealogy 40–49

Jessup, B. 7

Kimmelman, Gene 19
Kress, G. 6

land law 27
language 2–10, 29, 68, 80, 91, 92, 100; of law 2, 4, 30 (see also legal language)
Lazar, M. M. 54, 58, 81, 87
legal language 3, 5–7, 71

Machin, D. 82–83
MacLeod, N. J. 84
Magna Carta of Women (MCW) 52–59
Mayr, A. 82, 83
media markets 17, 21, 23
MeToo movement 96
Meyer, M. 82
Miller, M. K. 52
modern liberal constitutionalism 27
multi-directionality 53
multiple amicus briefs 22

national security 66, 70
negative consequences 93, 95, 97–100
nominal critique 98
nomination strategies 82–84

parliamentary debates 42, 44, 48
perpetrators 42, 87, 91, 94, 96, 97, 99, 100; mitigation 81, 82, 86, 87, 89
perspectivization strategies 85–86
Philippines 53, 55, 56, 58; women's rights law 53–54, 59
pluralism/plurality 29, 31–33, 49
Plurinational Constitutional Court (PCC) 27, 29, 30, 36
Plurinational Constitutional Judgment 29, 30, 34, 36
police interviews 10, 79–81
power relations 54, 78–80, 87, 89
practical reasoning 93
predication strategies 84–85

prototypes 5, 6
Public Order Act 10, 40, 42

race 7, 10, 40, 42, 43, 45–49, 79
Racial and Religious Hatred (RRH) Bill 42, 44, 47, 48
racial classification 35, 36
racial hatred 42, 45; offences 41, 45; provisions 41, 44, 45, 47
rape 80–82, 84, 86, 89, 91, 92; androcentric assumptions of 81
Reisigl, M. 29
religious hatred 42–44, 46–47; provisions 41, 43–45, 47–49
religious/religion 8, 10, 40, 42, 43, 45–47, 49; belief 43, 44, 46; groups 41, 45–49; identity 46, 48
reproductive health 10, 56, 58
reproductive rights 56, 57, 59
rhetorical/rhetoric 92, 93; analysis 92, 95; problems 45, 47
Richardson, J. 9
Roche, D. 65
Rubenstein, K. 7

Savery, L. 53
sequentiality 71, 72
settlement money 91, 93, 94, 96, 98, 99
sexual assault 78, 79, 82, 88, 89, 94–97
sexual violence 88, 91, 92, 94, 96, 97, 99, 100
Shalev, C. 58
South Korea 92, 94, 100
Steinbock, D. 66
substantive problem 46

tertiary text 41, 42, 47, 49
transitivity 81, 82, 86

Van Dijk, T. 5
Van Leeuwen, T. 65, 68, 72
Venema, R. M. 80
victimhood 99; stealing 99–100
victims 10, 42, 44, 81, 87, 91, 93, 95–100; blaming 79, 81, 82, 86, 87, 89
Vivir Bien: Bolivian constitution and 28–29; court's interpretation of constitutional principles of 30; principles of 27–36
Voorhoof, D. 8, 9

Walton, D. 93
Wodak, R. 29, 82
women's rights 54, 57, 58; law 53–54, 59
World Trade Organization (WTO) 4, 5, 9
Wright, R. F. 29

Yentl syndrome 78, 81

Zwingel, S. 52–53